CGP — the only logical choice...

The best way to get ready for the OCR GCSE Computer Science exams
is lots (and lots) of practice. That's where this brilliant CGP book comes in...

It's packed with hundreds of realistic exam-style questions, covering
everything from basic definitions to the dreaded 8-mark extended answers
— plus plenty of practice at writing code and algorithms.

And with step-by-step answers included at the back of the book,
you'll have compressed all the exam data into your memory in no time.

CGP — still the best! ☺

Our sole aim here at CGP is to produce the highest quality books —
carefully written, immaculately presented and dangerously close to being funny.

Then we work our socks off to get them out to you
— at the cheapest possible prices.

Contents

✓ Use the tick boxes to check off the topics you've completed.

Component 01 — Computer Systems

Section One — Components of a Computer System

Section Two — Networks

Section Three — Issues

Component 02 — Computational Thinking, Algorithms and Programming

Section Four — Algorithms

Section Five — Programming

Section Six — Design, Testing and IDEs

Section Seven — Data Representation

Published by CGP

Based on the classic CGP style created by Richard Parsons.

Editors: Liam Dyer, Rob Harrison, Shaun Harrogate, Simon Little and Jack Perry.

Contributor: Colin Harber-Stuart

With thanks to Lorna Bointon, Neil Hastings and Ali Mansour for the proofreading.

ISBN: 978 1 78294 603 8

Printed by Elanders Ltd, Newcastle upon Tyne
Clipart from Corel®

How to Use This Book

- Hold the book <u>upright</u>, approximately <u>50 cm</u> from your face, ensuring that the text looks like <u>this</u>, not ꙅᴉɥʇ. Alternatively, place the book on a <u>horizontal</u> surface (e.g. a table or desk) and sit adjacent to the book, at a distance which doesn't make the text too small to read.
- In case of emergency, press the two halves of the book together <u>firmly</u> in order to close.
- Before attempting to use this book, familiarise yourself with the following <u>safety information</u>:

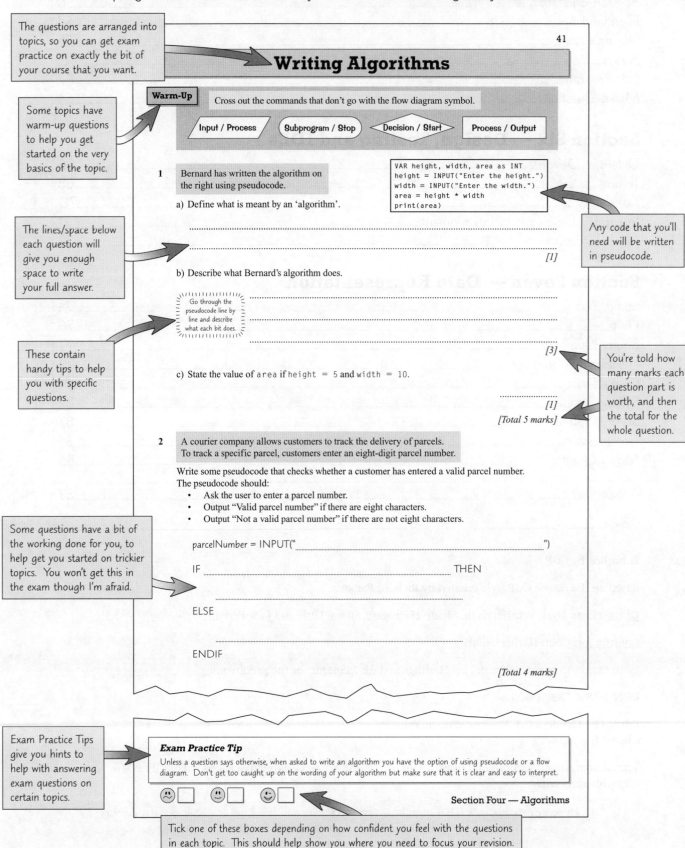

The questions are arranged into topics, so you can get exam practice on exactly the bit of your course that you want.

Some topics have warm-up questions to help you get started on the very basics of the topic.

The lines/space below each question will give you enough space to write your full answer.

These contain handy tips to help you with specific questions.

Some questions have a bit of the working done for you, to help get you started on trickier topics. You won't get this in the exam though I'm afraid.

Exam Practice Tips give you hints to help with answering exam questions on certain topics.

41

Writing Algorithms

Warm-Up   Cross out the commands that don't go with the flow diagram symbol.

Input / Process   Subprogram / Stop   Decision / Start   Process / Output

Any code that you'll need will be written in pseudocode.

1   Bernard has written the algorithm on the right using pseudocode.

```
VAR height, width, area as INT
height = INPUT("Enter the height.")
width = INPUT("Enter the width.")
area = height * width
print(area)
```

a) Define what is meant by an 'algorithm'.

....
....
[1]

b) Describe what Bernard's algorithm does.

Go through the pseudocode line by line and describe what each bit does.

....
....
....
[3]

c) State the value of area if height = 5 and width = 10.

....
[1]
[Total 5 marks]

You're told how many marks each question part is worth, and then the total for the whole question.

2   A courier company allows customers to track the delivery of parcels. To track a specific parcel, customers enter an eight-digit parcel number.

Write some pseudocode that checks whether a customer has entered a valid parcel number. The pseudocode should:
- Ask the user to enter a parcel number.
- Output "Valid parcel number" if there are eight characters.
- Output "Not a valid parcel number" if there are not eight characters.

parcelNumber = INPUT("...")

IF .... THEN

....

ELSE

....

ENDIF

[Total 4 marks]

Exam Practice Tip
Unless a question says otherwise, when asked to write an algorithm you have the option of using pseudocode or a flow diagram. Don't get too caught up on the wording of your algorithm but make sure that it is clear and easy to interpret.

☹ ☐   ☺ ☐   ☺ ☐

Section Four — Algorithms

Tick one of these boxes depending on how confident you feel with the questions in each topic. This should help show you where you need to focus your revision.

Exam Tips

Exam Stuff

1) You have to do <u>two exams</u> for your OCR GCSE in Computer Science — Components 01 and 02.

2) <u>Component 01</u> will focus on computer systems, networks and ethical, legal, cultural and environmental concerns. <u>Component 02</u> will focus on algorithms, programming, defensive design and logic.

3) Both exams are <u>1½ hours long</u>, and worth <u>80 marks</u>. Which means you should aim for a <u>mark per minute</u> and you'll have time to check back through your answers at the end.

4) You are <u>not allowed</u> to use a calculator for either exam.

There are a Few Golden Rules...

> Obeying these Golden Rules is no use if you haven't learnt the stuff in the first place. Make sure you revise well and do <u>as many</u> practice questions as you can.

1) **Always, always, always make sure you <u>read the question properly</u>.**
   E.g. if you're asked to convert your answer to binary, <u>don't</u> give it in denary.

2) **Look at the <u>number of marks</u> a question is worth.**
   The number of marks gives you a pretty good clue of <u>how much</u> to write. There's no point writing an essay for a question that's only worth one mark — it's just a waste of your time.

3) **Write your answers as <u>clearly</u> as you can.**
   If the examiner can't read your answer you won't get any marks, even if it's right.

4) **Use the <u>correct terminology</u>.**
   It's no good using <u>computery words</u> if you don't know what they mean — make sure you know your CPUs from your GPUs and your discs from your drives.

5) **Pay attention to the <u>time</u>.**
   If you're totally, hopelessly stuck on a question, just <u>leave it</u> and <u>move on</u> to the next one. You can always <u>go back to it</u> at the end if you've got enough time.

... and some extra tips for Certain Question Types

1) **Extended response questions.**
   Typically found at the end of component 01. To gain the <u>top marks</u> you'll need to show a <u>deep understanding</u> of the topic and give <u>accurate</u> and <u>detailed evidence</u> to back up your points.

2) **"Write an algorithm..." or "Write a sub program..."**
   These questions are common on component 02. There is <u>no strict format</u> for your answer — you can use <u>pseudocode</u>, a <u>flow diagram</u> or a <u>programming language</u>. But whichever format you choose, it must be <u>clear</u> to the examiner what each bit of your algorithm or sub program is doing.

You Need to Understand the Command Words

<u>Command words</u> are the words in a question that tell you <u>what to do</u>.
If you don't know what they mean, you might not be able to answer the questions properly.

State / Identify — You need to give a <u>short answer</u> (usually just a phrase or number) or <u>select an item</u> from a list of possible answers — no explanation is required.

Define — You need to give the <u>precise meaning</u> of a word, phrase or object.

Outline — You should give a <u>brief summary</u> of a process or concept.

Describe / Explain — You need to give a <u>detailed account</u> of a process or concept. For 'explain' questions you also need to give <u>reasons</u> or <u>causes</u>.

Discuss / Evaluate — You have to give a <u>balanced argument</u> covering a range of <u>opinions</u> and <u>arguments</u>, backing up each of your points with <u>evidence</u>.

Computer Systems

Warm-Up

Circle the items that are components of a computer system.

RAM   Graphics Card   Motherboard   A Dead Mouse

Hard Disk Drive   REM   Optical Drive   ROOM   The Internet   Heat Sink

Cooling Fan

1   Computer systems consist of hardware and software that work together.

a) Define what is meant by hardware. Give **one** example.

Definition: ....

Example: ....

[2]

b) Define what is meant by software. Give **one** example.

Definition: ....

Example: ....

[2]

[Total 4 marks]

2   A microwave contains an embedded system which controls its cooking modes.

a) What is an embedded system?

....

[1]

b) Give **two** other examples of devices that may contain an embedded system.

1 ....

2 ....

[2]

c) Explain **two** benefits of using an embedded system in a microwave instead of a general purpose computer.

1 ....

....

2 ....

....

[4]

[Total 7 marks]

The CPU

Write the names of the parts of the CPU in the correct places.

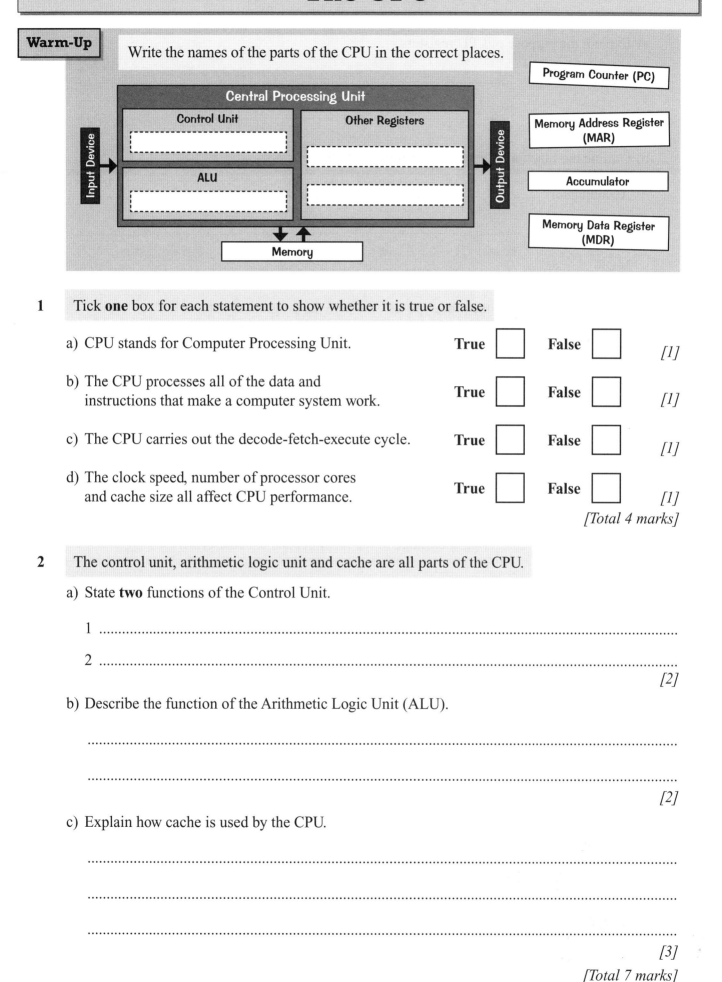

1 Tick **one** box for each statement to show whether it is true or false.

a) CPU stands for Computer Processing Unit. **True** ☐ **False** ☐ *[1]*

b) The CPU processes all of the data and
   instructions that make a computer system work. **True** ☐ **False** ☐ *[1]*

c) The CPU carries out the decode-fetch-execute cycle. **True** ☐ **False** ☐ *[1]*

d) The clock speed, number of processor cores
   and cache size all affect CPU performance. **True** ☐ **False** ☐ *[1]*

[Total 4 marks]

2 The control unit, arithmetic logic unit and cache are all parts of the CPU.

a) State **two** functions of the Control Unit.

1 ....

2 ....

[2]

b) Describe the function of the Arithmetic Logic Unit (ALU).

....

....

[2]

c) Explain how cache is used by the CPU.

....

....

....

[3]

[Total 7 marks]

Section One — Components of a Computer System

3 A tech firm have started producing their own CPUs.
They are currently testing the registers in some prototype CPUs.

a) Explain the purpose of CPU registers.

....

....

[2]

b) Outline the function of each of the following CPU registers:

Accumulator ....

MAR ....

MDR ....

[3]

c) A fault is identified in the prototype CPUs where the program counter is not
incrementing with each cycle. Explain what will happen in the CPU in this case.

....

....

[2]

[Total 7 marks]

4 CPUs process data according to the fetch-decode-execute cycle.

Describe what happens during each stage of the fetch-decode-execute cycle.

....

....

....

....

....

....

....

....

[Total 6 marks]

Exam Practice Tip

Whenever you're asked about the CPU it may help to visualise a diagram like the one on page 5. Make sure you know
what each acronym (e.g. ALU, MAR, MDR, PC) stands for, as this will give you a clue about what each bit does.

Section One — Components of a Computer System

Memory

1 Describe the difference between volatile and non-volatile memory.

....

....

[Total 2 marks]

2 Nigel runs a piece of software to analyse the performance of his computer.
It recommends that he should install more RAM in his computer.

a) Explain the purpose of RAM in a computer system.

....

....

[2]

b) Give **two** reasons why Nigel may need to install more RAM in his computer.

1 ....

2 ....

[2]

[Total 4 marks]

3 When a computer is switched on the BIOS runs. The BIOS is stored in the computer's ROM.

a) State **two** functions of the BIOS.

1 ....

2 ....

[2]

b) Explain why the BIOS is stored in ROM instead of RAM.

....

....

[2]

When many programs are running at once a computer may have to use virtual memory.

c) Explain how virtual memory works.

....

....

[2]

d) Explain **one** disadvantage of using virtual memory.

....

....

[2]

[Total 8 marks]

8

CPU and System Performance

1 Mary works as a graphic designer. For her latest project, she plans to upgrade her computer in order to run design software more smoothly.

Identify **three** components that could be upgraded to improve the performance of her computer.

1 ....

2 ....

3 ....

[Total 3 marks]

2 Jackson is considering upgrading his PC. Will offers to sell his old CPU to Jackson. Will's CPU is the same type as Jackson's CPU but has a different specification.

Jackson's CPU	Will's CPU
8 cores	4 cores
6 MB cache	3 MB cache
1.6 GHz clock speed	2.8 GHz clock speed

a) Define the term clock speed.

....

[1]

b) Explain why using a CPU with a large cache capacity may increase CPU performance.

....

....

[2]

c) Do you think Jackson should buy Will's CPU? Give reasons to justify your decision.

....

....

....

....

[4]

d) Jackson decides to increase the RAM in his PC from 4 GB to 8 GB.
He was disappointed to find no noticeable increase in his computer's performance.
Explain why this may be the case.

....

....

[2]

[Total 9 marks]

Secondary Storage

Warm-Up

Match each sentence to the correct storage device.

Suitcase

Hard Disk Drive

Magnetic Tape

Uses a type of flash memory.

Data is stored on a stack of magnetic disks.

Data is stored as little pits on the surface.

Usually comes on a reel in a casette.

Floppy disk

Solid State Drive

Optical Disc

1 Shaun is going on a two week skiing trip. Each night, he will copy photos and videos to his laptop's secondary storage.

a) Give **three** characteristics to consider when choosing a suitable type of secondary storage for a computer system.

1 ....

2 ....

3 ....

[3]

b) Shaun will be using a helmet-mounted action camera to record videos whilst skiing. The camera records video onto a flash memory card.

i) Give **two** reasons why flash memory is a suitable storage type for an action camera.

1 ....

2 ....

[2]

ii) Explain why a magnetic hard disk would be an unsuitable storage type for an action camera.

....

....

[2]

[Total 7 marks]

2 Caley is getting a custom-built computer. She has a choice of two options for secondary storage: A 500 GB HDD (10 000 rpm) or a 128 GB SSD. For each storage option, give reasons why Caley may choose it over the other option.

500 GB HDD ....

....

128 GB SSD ....

....

[Total 4 marks]

3 Every night a large law firm backs up roughly 600 GB of data. At the end of each month, one final backup is taken and stored permanently, and the daily backups are deleted.

a) After three weeks, how much data will they have from daily backups? Give your answer in TB.

....

[1]

b) Circle a suitable storage type to store the daily backups from the choices below.

Hard Disk Drive   Magnetic Tape   Solid State Drive   Optical Disk

[1]

c) Outline the advantages and disadvantages of using your choice in part b) for data backups.

Advantages ....

....

Disadvantages ....

....

[4]

[Total 6 marks]

4 Jason has bought a new laptop.
The laptop contains 3 GB RAM and 128 GB secondary storage.

a) Explain why secondary storage is needed in addition to RAM.

....

....

....

....

[3]

Jason wants to back up the data on his laptop twice a week.

b) Give **two** advantages and **two** disadvantages of storing his backup data on optical discs.

Advantages 1 ....

2 ....

Disadvantages 1 ....

2 ....

[4]

[Total 7 marks]

Exam Practice Tip
Make sure you can rhyme off all the advantages and disadvantages for each type of secondary storage.
Consider the speed, capacity, cost and the various characteristics of each storage device, e.g. reliability and portability.

Systems Software

Warm-Up

Warm-Up   Find the names of **five** operating systems below.

```
E  M  J  R  C  O  D  E  R  D  A  I  K  Y  S  E
F  L  E  G  I  M  R  B  N  Z  B  O  V  I  A  U
W  I  F  M  E  A  N  D  R  O  I  D  A  O  L  M
A  N  T  B  Q  C  C  E  R  I  H  T  I  S  R  T
R  U  S  E  H  O  D  W  I  N  D  O  W  S  D  S
D  X  F  U  H  S  D  G  T  B  N  I  R  T  Z  B
```

1   David has just installed a new operating system on his computer.

a) State **three** functions of an operating system.

1 ....

2 ....

3 ....

[3]

After the new OS was installed, it automatically downloaded and installed the device drivers.

b) Describe what is meant by device drivers.

....

....

[2]

c) Identify **two** features the operating system may provide to help protect David's personal data.

1 ....

2 ....

[2]

[Total 7 marks]

2   Josephine's computer has a multi-tasking operating system. Explain how the operating system manages memory and CPU time to allow the computer to multi-task.

....

....

....

....

....

....

[Total 6 marks]

3   Selina has customised the graphical user interface (GUI) on her computer's operating system.

a) Describe the purpose of a graphical user interface.

....

....
[2]

b) Selina's operating system also has an optional command line interface.
   i) Define what is meant by a command line interface.

   ....
   [1]

   ii) Identify **two** benefits of using a command line interface instead of a GUI.

   1 ....

   2 ....
   [2]

c) The operating system includes an encryption utility that can be used to encrypt folders and files. Explain **one** reason why Selina may use the encryption utility.

....

....
[2]

[Total 7 marks]

4   An accounting firm plans to introduce a new scheme for regularly backing up its data.

a) Define what is meant by the following types of backup.

Full backup ....

Incremental backup ....
[2]

b) Describe a possible backup scheme for the firm that includes:
   - full backups   • incremental backups
   - data compression   • security measures

....

....

....

....

....
[4]

[Total 6 marks]

5   Annie has a three year old laptop. She is giving the laptop a full service before selling it on.

a) Annie runs some 'Disk Health' utility software to check for any problems with her HDD.

   i)   Define what is meant by utility software.

   ....

   [1]

   ii) Give **two** other examples of utility software.

   1 ....

   2 ....

   [2]

b) The 'Disk Health' utility recommends performing a disk clean-up to remove unnecessary files.
   Suggest **two** types of files that might be removed during the clean-up process.

   1 ....

   2 ....

   [2]

c) The utility also reports that Annie's hard disk is 25% fragmented.

   i)   Describe how a hard disk can become fragmented over time.

   ....

   ....

   ....

   [3]

   ii) Explain **one** problem caused by a fragmented hard disk.

   ....

   ....

   [2]

   iii) Briefly describe the defragmentation process.

   ....

   ....

   ....

   [3]

   iv) Suggest why it could be better to do the disk clean-up
        before defragmentation rather than afterwards.

   ....

   [1]

   [Total 14 marks]

Open Source and Proprietary Software

Warm-Up   Circle the open source software and underline the proprietary software below.

Android™   Linux   Adobe® Photoshop®   Mozilla® Firefox®

Microsoft® PowerPoint®   VLC   Spandau Ballet   Microsoft® Word

1   A marketing company has the same, paid-for, proprietary software on all of its computers.
The software provides facilities for word processing, presentations, spreadsheets and databases.

a) Describe what is meant by proprietary software.

....

....
[2]

b) Identify **two** advantages and **two** disadvantages to the company of using proprietary software.

Advantages 1 ....

2 ....

Disadvantages 1 ....

2 ....
[4]

[Total 6 marks]

2   Ioteck has created TV-PCs. TV-PCs plug into any
USB-compatible TV, and come packaged with a
selection of open source software.

TV-PC *Only £39.99!*
**Turn your TV into a PC for
word processing, spreadsheets,
slideshows, databases and photos!**
*Includes portable projector-keyboard
— type on any surface!*
NEW

a) Describe what is meant by open source software.

....

....
[2]

b) Explain **one** advantage and **one** disadvantage to Ioteck
of using open source software on the TV-PCs.

Advantage ....

....

Disadvantage ....

....
[4]

[Total 6 marks]

Section One — Components of a Computer System

Mixed Questions

1 Hardeep wants to try a new operating system on his computer.
The new operating system is optimised for use with a touchscreen.

	Hardeep's PC	**OS Minimum Requirements**
Processor:	2.1 GHz, 4 cores	1.0 GHz, 4 cores
RAM:	2 GB	2 GB
Storage:	256 GB, 125 MB free	19 GB free space
GPU:	Integrated 256 MB	Dedicated 512 MB

a) Hardeep needs to upgrade some of the components in his computer before the new
operating system can be installed. State which components must be upgraded.

1 ....

2 ....

[2]

b) Would you recommend that Hardeep upgrades any other components in his computer?
Explain your answer.

....

....

[2]

c) Explain why an operating system requires a certain amount of RAM.

....

....

[2]

d) The new operating system's GUI is optimised for touchscreen use.
Describe **two** features that a GUI may include to take advantage of touchscreen technology.

1 ....

....

2 ....

....

[4]

e) Various applications on Hardeep's computer need to be updated to run on the new OS.
After the update, Hardeep notices that one application saves files with a different
file extension to the older version. Explain the purpose of a file extension.

....

....

[2]

[Total 12 marks]

16

2 Three computers are on sale in a computer store. Their specifications are shown below.

	CGPC3000	XZ Monochrome	CGPC-Pro
CPU	Ioteck S44: Quad-core, 2.4 GHz, 4 MB cache	Ioteck X3: Octa-core, 3.3 GHz, 6 MB cache	Ioteck S30: Dual-core, 2.4 GHz, 2 MB cache
RAM	4 GB	8 GB	4 GB
Storage	1 TB HDD (5400 rpm)	500 GB SSD	128 GB HDD (7200 rpm)
Graphics	Integrated 512 MB	Ioteck UltraBurst 2 GB	Integrated 512 MB
OS	Legacy 3	Legacy 3	Legacy 3
Price	£300	£650	£200

a) Kirstie and Liam go shopping for computers. They each have different requirements but don't want to spend more money than is necessary.

i) Kirstie needs a computer for word processing, emailing, downloading high definition TV series from an online store and basic photo editing.
Which computer would you recommend for Kirstie? Give reasons for your answer.

....

....

....

....

[4]

ii) Liam wants to replace his old video games console with a new gaming PC. He wants to be able to play the latest games releases, but will also need his computer for browsing the Internet, and editing databases. Which computer would you recommend for him?
Give reasons for your answer.

....

....

....

....

[4]

b) Liam decides to overclock the CPU on his new computer.
Explain **one** positive and **one** negative effect that overclocking the CPU may have.

Positive ....

....

Negative ....

....

[4]

[Total 12 marks]

Networks — LANs and WANs

1   In an office there are six computers, a scanner and a router connected together in a Local Area Network (LAN).

a) Define the term Local Area Network (LAN).

....

[1]

b) State **three** advantages of connecting the computers together into a Local Area Network.

1   ....

2   ....

3   ....

[3]

[Total 4 marks]

2   Dishley Academy is connected to other schools in the area using a Wide Area Network (WAN).

Hint: WANs connect LANs.

a) Describe what is meant by a Wide Area Network (WAN).

....

....

[2]

b) Explain **two** of the potential benefits of using a WAN to connect the Academy to other schools.

1   ....

....

2   ....

....

[4]

c) Explain **three** factors that can affect the performance of a network.

1   ....

....

2   ....

....

3   ....

....

[6]

[Total 12 marks]

Networks — Hardware

Warm-Up Draw a line between the name and the matching definition.

Wi-Fi® channel	A type of copper cable that consists of a central wire protected by a metal shield.
Coaxial cable	Contains twisted pairs of copper wires.
CAT5e cable	A type of cable that uses light to carry signals.
Fibre optic cable	A range of Wi-Fi® frequencies.

1 Jane works from home. She connects her laptop and television to her home Local Area Network (LAN). Jane uses a home router to connect her LAN together.

a) State the name of the hardware device inside the laptop that connects it to the LAN.

....

[1]

b) Jane can connect her devices to the router using either Ethernet or Wi-Fi®.

　i) State how an Ethernet connection is different to a Wi-Fi® connection.

....

[1]

　ii) Jane's television lacks any wireless capability. State the name of the hardware Jane can use to allow her television to connect to the LAN wirelessly.

....

[1]

c) Jane's home router functions as a switch, router and Wireless Access Point (WAP) all in one. Outline the function of each of these devices.

　i) Switch

....

....

[2]

　ii) Router

....

....

[2]

　iii) Wireless Access Point (WAP)

....

....

[2]

[Total 9 marks]

Client-Server and Peer-to-Peer Networks

Put the numbers 1 to 5 in each of the boxes below
to show the correct order of a Client-Server request.

☐ The web server sends the web page data to the web browser.

☐ The web server processes the request.

☐ The web browser displays the web page for the user to view.

☐ The user clicks on a web page link in their web browser.

☐ The web browser asks the web server to send the web page data.

1 Bill's graphic design business has ten members of staff, each with their own
computer. The staff work together by sharing files between their computers.

a) The staff's computers are connected together in a Peer-to-Peer (P2P) network.

   i) Describe what is meant by a Peer-to-Peer (P2P) network.

   ....

   ....

   [2]

   ii) Identify **two** benefits and **two** drawbacks of using a Peer-to-Peer (P2P) network.

   Benefits 1 ....

              2 ....

   Drawbacks 1 ....

                2 ....

   [4]

b) An IT consultant suggests the company should adopt a Client-Server network setup.

   i) Describe what is meant by a Client-Server network.

   ....

   ....

   [2]

   ii) Identify **two** benefits and **two** drawbacks of changing from a Peer-to-Peer (P2P) network to
   a Client-Server network.

   Benefits 1 ....

              2 ....

   Drawbacks 1 ....

                2 ....

   [4]

   [Total 12 marks]

Network Topologies

1 A leisure centre has a Local Area Network (LAN) consisting of five computers and a central server connected in a star topology.

a) Draw a diagram of the leisure centre's star network.

[2]

b) Identify **three** advantages of the star topology.

A good way to think about the advantages of a star topology is to compare it to a bus or ring topology.

1 ....

2 ....

3 ....

[3]

[Total 5 marks]

2 The table below shows star topologies, partial mesh topologies and full mesh topologies for different numbers of nodes.

Nodes are the dots on the diagrams used to represent network devices.

a) Complete the table by correctly connecting the nodes in the white cells.

Number of nodes	Star	Partial Mesh	Full Mesh
4			
5			
6			

[4]

b) Explain **one** advantage and **one** disadvantage of mesh topologies compared to star topologies.

Advantage ....

....

Disadvantage ....

....

[4]

[Total 8 marks]

3 A company has its employees' computers spread across four floors. The computers on each floor are connected to that floor's server in a star network. Employees need to access files on all of the servers, so each of the four servers are connected in another star network, with a central switch located on the ground floor.

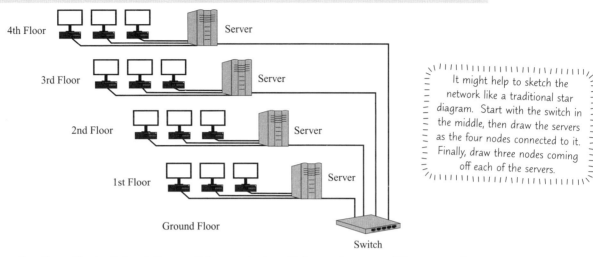

> It might help to sketch the network like a traditional star diagram. Start with the switch in the middle, then draw the servers as the four nodes connected to it. Finally, draw three nodes coming off each of the servers.

a) Describe the effect of the failure of the central switch on the rest of the network.

....

....

[2]

b) The company decides to remove the switch from the network and instead connect the four servers in a full mesh network, as shown in this diagram.

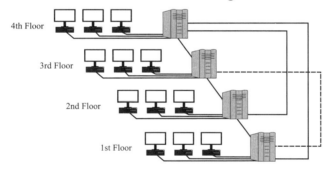

Explain the advantages and disadvantages to the company of connecting the servers together in a full mesh network instead of a star network.

....

....

....

....

....

[4]

[Total 6 marks]

Exam Practice Tip

Make sure you get to grips with what each different network topology looks like. Remember: a full mesh is when all devices are directly connected to each other, while devices in a partial mesh are only indirectly connected.

Network Protocols

1 Data is sent over the Internet using packet switching, which follows certain network protocols.

a) Define the term network protocol.

....

[1]

b) The sentences below describe the packet switching sequence. Fill in the missing words.

- The sending device splits the data up into smaller units called ....
- Each packet is given a .... to show the order of the data.
- The direction each packet takes to reach its destination is decided by pieces of hardware called .... using the .... protocol.
- Packets sometimes arrive at the receiving device in the wrong order. The receiving device uses the .... to put them in the right order.

[5]

[Total 6 marks]

2 Mahindar sends an email to Jonathan over the Internet using his smartphone. Jonathan receives the email on his laptop.

a) Explain why Mahindar and Jonathan's devices need IP addresses to connect to the Internet.

....

....

[2]

b) Mahindar's email is split into packets and sent over the network using packet switching. Outline the possible actions of Jonathan's laptop and Mahindar's smartphone when:

   i)   one of the packets is lost in transit.

....

....

....

[3]

   ii) one of the packets is corrupted in transit.

....

....

....

[3]

[Total 8 marks]

3 The table below shows the names and functions of different network protocols.

Complete the missing spaces in the table.

Remember that each of these protocols does a specific task on networks like the Internet. Some have similar jobs but handle them slightly differently.

Protocol	Function
TCP	
	Responsible for packet switching.
HTTP	
	A more secure version of HTTP.
FTP	
SMTP	
	Used to retrieve emails from a server. The user downloads a copy of the email and the server holds the original email until the user deletes it.
	Used to retrieve emails from a server. The server holds the email until the user downloads it, at which point the server deletes it.

[Total 8 marks]

4 Sally works in an office. Her computer has a MAC address, which helps Sally to access files from the company's server.

Don't confuse a MAC address with an IP address.

a) Describe what is meant by a MAC address.

....

....
[2]

b) The network managers at Sally's company work with layers of network protocols.

  i) Describe what is meant by a layer of network protocols.

....

....
[2]

  ii) State the name of **one** layer of network protocols and outline its function.

Layer name: ....

Layer function: ....
[2]

  iii) Identify **three** benefits of using layers when working with network protocols.

1 ....

2 ....

3 ....
[3]

[Total 9 marks]

24

Networks — The Internet

Warm-Up

Draw lines between the labels and the part of the URL they describe.

https://www.cgpbooks.co.uk/student/books_gcse

| Path to the specific page | | Protocol | | Domain name |

1 The Internet offers access to a variety of services, including the World Wide Web.

a) Explain the difference between the Internet and the World Wide Web.

....

[2]

b) State the function of a Domain Name Server (DNS).

....

[1]

[Total 3 marks]

2 A marketing company's employees regularly travel between sites in London and Doha. The managers want to establish a Virtual Private Network (VPN) for the company.

a) Describe what is meant by a virtual network.

....

....

[2]

b) Explain how the company could make use of a Virtual Private Network (VPN).

....

....

[2]

[Total 4 marks]

3 A magazine publishing company based in rural Scotland connect their computers in a LAN using a Client-Server setup. Their writers live elsewhere in the UK and either email or post their articles to the company, where they are edited in time for the weekly deadline.

Discuss the advantages and disadvantages to the company of changing from their current system to one which uses the cloud.

....

....

....

....

[Total 6 marks]

Section Two — Networks

Network Security Threats

Warm-Up

Draw lines between the type of malware and its description.

Ransomware	Alters permissions and access levels on the user's device.
Virus	Tells the user their computer is infected with malware in order to make them follow malicious links to "fix" the problem.
Rootkit	Self-replicating malware.
Spyware	Secretly monitors user actions.
Trojan	Encrypts the data on the user's device, making them pay money to the hacker in exchange for the key to decrypt it.
Scareware	Spread by users copying infected files.
Worm	Malware disguised as legitimate software.

1   National Lending Bank stores the banking data of thousands of customers. The bank has recently suffered a passive attack, where customer data was stolen, and a denial-of-service attack.

a) i)   Define the term passive attack.

....

[1]

    ii)   State **one** way of preventing a passive attack.

....

[1]

b) Explain what is meant by a denial-of-service attack.

....

....

[2]

c) As a result of recent attacks, the bank is planning to carry out a pentest on the network. Explain how pentesting is used to improve network security.

....

....

[2]

[Total 6 marks]

2 Hannah regularly receives fake emails claiming to be from well-known banks and other organisations.

> These types of emails are a form of social engineering.

a) State the name given to the practice of sending fake or spoof emails.

....

[1]

b) Explain the purpose of these fake emails.

....

....

[2]

c) Hannah also receives suspicious emails that contain attachments, sometimes from names in her own contacts list. Explain the dangers of opening untrusted email attachments.

....

....

[2]

[Total 5 marks]

3 Kate is a network administrator at a secondary school. She has put in place measures to prevent attacks on the school's network, including firewalls and different user access levels.

a) Explain how a firewall can prevent attacks on the school's network.

....

....

[2]

b) Explain why the school's network needs to have different user access levels.

....

....

....

[3]

c) A hacker recently broke through the school's network security using a brute force attack.

   i) Explain what is meant by a brute force attack.

....

....

[2]

   ii) Identify **two** steps the school can take to protect against a brute force attack.

   1 ....

   2 ....

[2]

[Total 9 marks]

4 A supermarket sells its products online. It stores user account information in a database which is accessed when the customer places an order. The supermarket recently suffered a security breach in which the data of thousands of customers was stolen.

a) A common way for databases to be breached is through SQL injection.

i) Explain how SQL injection works.

....

....

[2]

ii) Explain how SQL injection attacks can be prevented.

....

....

[2]

b) The supermarket believes the data was stolen through social engineering.
Describe an example of how the thieves could have used social engineering to steal the data.

....

....

[2]

[Total 6 marks]

5 A law firm has 100 members of staff in an office building in London. The firm stores confidential data about its clients on a server. The firm currently has no network policy.

Discuss how a network policy could benefit the law firm.

Consider the threats posed to the firm's network and how a network policy could prevent them.

....

....

....

....

....

....

....

....

....

....

[Total 8 marks]

Exam Practice Tip

Out there in the real world it's not enough to name types of attacks — you need to know how to prevent them as well. The same is true of the exam — for every possible threat you can think of, keep in mind a prevention method for it too.

Mixed Questions

1 A Yorkshire-based television company has two studios, one based in Leeds and the other based in York. The company's computer network is shown in the diagram below.

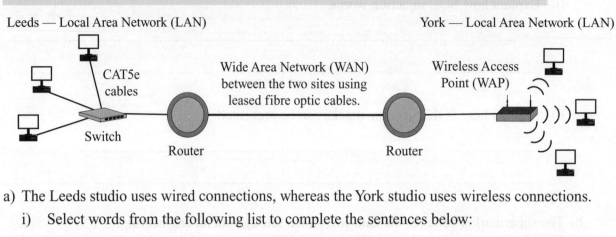

a) The Leeds studio uses wired connections, whereas the York studio uses wireless connections.

   i) Select words from the following list to complete the sentences below:

   Ethernet   **WPA2**   **WAP**   **Coaxial**   **SQL**   **Frame**

   .... is a network protocol used on wired networks.

   .... is a security protocol used on wireless LANs.

   [2]

   ii) Describe **one** difference between a CAT5e twisted pair cable and a coaxial cable.

   ....

   ....

   [2]

   iii) Outline the advantages and disadvantages of each LAN setup.

   The Leeds studio's wired setup: ....

   ....

   ....

   The York studio's wireless setup: ....

   ....

   ....

   [4]

b) The studios are connected in a Wide Area Network (WAN) using fibre optic cables.

   i) State **one** advantage of using fibre optic cables rather than copper cables in a WAN.

   ....

   [1]

   ii) Identify **one** reason why the company uses leased lines for its WAN.

   ....

   [1]

   [Total 10 marks]

2 Karen stores her holiday pictures in the cloud. She decides to download an image from the cloud to her laptop.

a) Define what is meant by the cloud.

....
[1]

b) Karen's laptop and the cloud server have a client-server relationship. Describe the communication that takes place between the cloud server and Karen's laptop when she downloads the image.

....

....
[2]

c) The image is transferred from the cloud server to Karen's laptop using packets.
   i) Explain how packets are used to transfer the image over the Internet to Karen's laptop.

....

....

....

....

....

....

....
[6]

   ii) Explain why packet switching is an efficient way to send data over large networks.

....

....
[2]

d) The cloud hosting company uses a system of network forensics as part of its network policy.
   i) Define the term network policy.

....
[1]

   ii) Explain what is meant by network forensics and how they are used.

....

....

....

....
[3]

[Total 15 marks]

Section Two — Networks

Ethical and Cultural Issues

Warm-Up

Tick one box in each row to show whether it concerns censorship or surveillance.

	Censorship	Surveillance
A business monitors what their employees view online.		
A country's government blocks access to Facebook®.		
A government agency intercepts emails containing certain words.		
A school restricts access to harmful websites.		
An Internet Service Provider collects data on browsing habits.		

1   A supermarket replaces all of their staffed checkouts with electronic self-service checkouts. The owners of the supermarket notice an increase in profits, but employees who work on the checkouts lose their jobs.

a) Define the term stakeholder.

....

[1]

b) Identify **two** stakeholders in the decision to replace the staffed checkouts. State whether the effect on these stakeholders was positive or negative and give a reason for your answer.

Stakeholder 1: ....

The effect on this stakeholder was: Positive / Negative

Reason: ....

Stakeholder 2: ....

The effect on this stakeholder was: Positive / Negative

Reason: ....

[6]

[Total 7 marks]

2   Identify **two** health risks caused by using technology. State how each could be prevented.

Health risk: ....

Prevention: ....

Health risk: ....

Prevention: ....

[Total 4 marks]

3   Jasmine uses several social media websites.
Jasmine was a recent victim of cyberbullying.

a) Define the terms cyberbullying and trolling.

Cyberbullying: ....

Trolling: ....

[2]

b) Suggest **two** reasons why cyberbullying and trolling have become a problem on social media.

1 ....

2 ....

[2]

c) Describe **one** example of how social media can affect the privacy of those who use it.

....

....

[2]

d) Social media has also had a positive impact on how we communicate.
Describe **one** way in which social media benefits its users.

....

....

[2]

[Total 8 marks]

4   Some businesses restrict and monitor what their employees view online.

a) Discuss the impact of the increasing use of censorship software in the workplace.

....

....

....

....

[4]

b) Discuss the ethical issues of employers monitoring what their employees are viewing online.

....

....

....

....

[4]

[Total 8 marks]

Section Three — Issues

5   Tom works for a smartphone company. Tom is stressed because he feels he can never switch off from work.

a) Explain how new technology could have allowed work to intrude into other areas of Tom's life.

....

....

[2]

b) Tom's company releases a new smartphone every year.
Outline the social pressures that can be created by the regular release of new technology.

....

....

[2]

c) Tom's neighbour, Jerry, is stressed because he is finding it difficult to apply for jobs. All the companies he wants to apply to only accept online applications, and he has limited access to the Internet. Explain **one** reason why somebody might only have a limited access to the Internet.

....

....

[2]

[Total 6 marks]

6   In many factories robots have replaced humans for routine tasks such as cutting and joining materials together and retrieving products stored in a warehouse.

Discuss the impact of robots replacing humans to carry out routine tasks in factories.

In your answer you might consider: stakeholders, technology and ethical issues.

....

....

....

....

....

....

....

....

[Total 6 marks]

> ***Exam Practice Tip***
> There's rarely a right or wrong answer to these issues, so expect the exam to use them in longer discussion questions, not just knowledge testing. These high mark questions will often give a real-life situation. When you're backing up points with examples or evidence, make sure it's all relevant to the situation you're given — so don't write about killer intelligent toasters unless the situation you're given is about the threats of using AI in kitchen appliances...

Environmental Issues

Warm-Up

Circle the words below that are the names of materials used in electronic devices.

Jupiter   Plastic   Mercury   Silver

Platinum   Potato   Gold

Copper   Cedar wood   Mithril   Fancyshinyinium

1   Modern devices contain a range of different raw materials.

a) Define the term raw material.

....

[1]

b) Identify **two** effects that the use of raw materials for electronic devices has on the environment.

1 ....

2 ....

[2]

[Total 3 marks]

2   The average smartphone is only used for two years before it is discarded as e-waste.

a) Define the term e-waste.

....

[1]

b) Identify **two** reasons why smartphones are only used for a short amount of time before they are discarded.

1 ....

2 ....

[2]

c) Outline the problems that the short life span of many electronic devices has on the environment.

....

....

....

....

[4]

d) Outline how the problem of e-waste can be managed to limit its impact on the environment.

....

....

[2]

[Total 9 marks]

3 The average household can spend almost £100 a year on wasted electricity.

a) Identify **two** ways that electronic devices waste electricity.

1 ....

2 ....

[2]

b) Explain how hardware manufacturers can limit the amount of electricity
wasted by electronic devices.

....

....

[2]

c) Briefly discuss the challenges in meeting the increasing worldwide demand for electricity.

....

....

....

....

[4]

[Total 8 marks]

4 Shaun has had his computer monitor for two years and
it still works. He would like to throw away the monitor
and replace it with a new, more energy efficient model.

> Think about Shaun's decision
> in terms of energy, e-waste
> and natural resources.

Discuss the environmental impact of Shaun's decision to replace his
current monitor with one which is more energy efficient.

....

....

....

....

....

....

....

[Total 6 marks]

Exam Practice Tip

It's useful to remember that almost everything has some sort of environmental effect. Take a look at question 6 on
page 32 — using robots in the workplace has a load of environmental impacts on top of all the ethical issues. Some
questions might even ask about both ethical and environmental issues, so try to get used to writing about them together.

Computer Legislation

Warm-Up

Draw a line between each issue and the law that it would apply to.

A hospital holds the medical records of its patients so they can be treated.

A criminal hacks into a broadband company's network and steals its customers' account details.

A request is made to a university to release information regarding the amount their vice chancellor is paid.

A polling company holds data on members of the public for a survey it is conducting.

An employee accesses their manager's network account and deletes company data.

Computer Misuse Act 1990

Data Protection Act 1998

Freedom of Information Act 2000

1 The Data Protection Act 1998 gives rights to data subjects.

a) Define the term data subject.

....

[1]

b) State **three** principles of the Data Protection Act.

E.g. one of the DPA's principles is that data held by an organisation must be kept accurate and up to date.

1 ....

2 ....

3 ....

[3]

[Total 4 marks]

2 Illegal file sharers infringe upon the copyright of musicians and film makers.

a) Define the term copyright.

....

[1]

b) Some pieces of music are in the public domain. Explain what is meant by the public domain.

....

....

[2]

[Total 3 marks]

3 Hayley is creating a website with information on her local town and its sports teams.

a) Hayley wishes to use a photograph that she has found on another website. The image has been copyrighted. Outline what Hayley needs to do if she wishes to use the photograph legally.

....

....

....

....

[3]

b) Hayley has taken a photograph that she wishes to use on her website. She would like to obtain a Creative Commons licence for her photograph. Explain why a photographer might choose a Creative Commons licence instead of a traditional "all rights reserved" copyright licence.

....

....

[2]

c) Each Creative Commons licence comes with certain conditions that describe how the intellectual property can be shared. State what each of these conditions means.

   i) Attribution

....

[1]

   ii) Non-commercial

....

[1]

   iii) Share-alike

....

[1]

   iv) No derivative works

....

[1]

d) Hayley decides to obtain a combined Attribution, Non-commercial and Share-alike licence. Several weeks later, she finds that her photograph is being used to advertise a local solicitor, with no copyright information or acknowledgement found anywhere on the advertisement. Explain **two** ways that the solicitor has infringed upon Hayley's copyright.

   1 ....

....

   2 ....

....

[4]

[Total 13 marks]

Section Three — Issues

4 A member of the public has sent a Freedom of Information request to their local council.

a) Outline how the local council should respond to the request.

....

....

[2]

b) The local council's computer network was recently hacked. The stolen data included sensitive information about members of the public, some of whom had left the area years ago.
Explain the legal issues for both the hackers and the local council.

....

....

....

....

....

....

[4]
[Total 6 marks]

5 A cinema collects information from customers who book seats to watch movies.
The cinema would like to store this information for the following reasons:
 • to make it easier for customers when they book seats in the future.
 • to enable the cinema to contact customers with details of future films.

Explain the measures that the cinema should take to ensure that customer data is stored legally.

....

....

....

....

....

....

....

[Total 6 marks]

Exam Practice Tip

For the longer questions, don't just write down everything you know about that topic — all the points you make should be directly relevant to the question. Planning your answer or jotting down a few notes beforehand can help you with this. The question may even suggest points for you to cover — use them to make sure you're answering the question.

Mixed Questions

1   Satellite navigation systems are used by many car and lorry
drivers to enable them to plan and follow a route to their destination.

Discuss the impact of the increasing use of satellite navigation systems to plan journeys. In your
answer you might consider: stakeholders, technology, ethical issues and environmental issues.

....

....

....

....

....

....

....

[Total 6 marks]

2   Many people today use social media to communicate with their friends.

Discuss the impact of the use of social media to communicate and share information.
In your answer you might consider: technology, ethical issues, privacy issues and cultural issues.

....

....

....

....

....

....

....

....

....

....

....

[Total 8 marks]

3   Smartphones can now be used instead of notes,
coins or bank cards when making purchases in a shop.

Discuss the impact of the increasing use of smartphones as a replacement to traditional forms
of payment. In your answer you might consider: stakeholders, technology, ethical issues and
environmental issues.

....

....

....

....

....

....

....

[Total 6 marks]

4   Recent years have seen the increasing use of computer technology
to distribute and view digital media content (music, movies and books).

Discuss the impact of the increasing use of digital media. In your answer you
might consider: stakeholders, technology, environmental issues and legal issues.

....

....

....

....

....

....

....

....

....

....

....

[Total 8 marks]

Section Three — Issues

Computational Thinking

Use the correct words to complete the sentences below.

solving
complex
abstraction
important
details
information
individually

Decomposition is breaking down a ......complex...... problem into smaller problems and .... each one ....

.... is picking out the .... bits of .... from the problem, ignoring the specific .... that don't matter.

1 A hardware company plans to make a computer keyboard for Greek language students.

a) Complete the missing rows in the table below to show the decomposition and abstraction steps the hardware company might take when making the keyboard.

Decomposition	Abstraction	
Things to look at	Details to ignore	Details to focus on
What keys are needed?	Letters from other alphabets.	Letters from the Greek alphabet.

[4]

b) Define what is meant by algorithmic thinking.

....

[1]

[Total 5 marks]

2 A file uploading service won't allow two files with the same file name to be uploaded. If a file name already exists, it will ask the user to change the file name.

a) Describe with examples how abstraction can help decide how to compare the files.

....

....

....

[3]

b) Describe with examples how decomposition could be used to help program this task.

....

....

....

[3]

[Total 6 marks]

Writing Algorithms

Cross out the commands that don't go with the flow diagram symbol.

Input / Process   Subprogram / Stop   Decision / Start   Process / Output

1   Bernard has written the algorithm on the right using pseudocode.

```
VAR height, width, area as INT
height = INPUT("Enter the height.")
width = INPUT("Enter the width.")
area = height * width
print(area)
```

a) Define what is meant by an 'algorithm'.

....
....

[1]

b) Describe what Bernard's algorithm does.

Go through the pseudocode line by line and describe what each bit does.

....
....
....

[3]

c) State the value of area if height = 5 and width = 10.

....

[1]

[Total 5 marks]

2   A courier company allows customers to track the delivery of parcels.
To track a specific parcel, customers enter an eight-digit parcel number.

Write some pseudocode that checks whether a customer has entered a valid parcel number.
The pseudocode should:
   • Ask the user to enter a parcel number.
   • Output "Valid parcel number" if there are eight characters.
   • Output "Not a valid parcel number" if there are not eight characters.

parcelNumber = INPUT("..")

IF .... THEN

....

ELSE

....

ENDIF

[Total 4 marks]

3 The flow diagram below shows how to convert miles to kilometres.

INPUT miles → kilometres = miles * 8/5 → OUTPUT kilometres

a) Identify **one** problem with this flow diagram.

....

[1]

b) State the distance in kilometres of 10 miles.

.... km

[1]

c) Draw an improved flow diagram by:
   - Using a more accurate conversion factor of 1.6093 instead of 8/5.
   - Asking the user if they wish to convert another distance.
     If yes, the flow diagram performs the new calculation and if not, the flow diagram ends.

[5]

[Total 7 marks]

4 At Tom's Tombola, every ticket number ending in either a 5 or a 0 is a winning ticket.

a) Complete the flow diagram below to show a ticket number as an input and whether it is a winning ticket as an output.

Start → INPUT ticketNumber

[4]

The flow diagram in part a) can be represented by this sub routine: | ticket |

b) Use | ticket | to draw a second flow diagram for someone picking 10 tickets.

[6]

[Total 10 marks]

Section Four — Algorithms

5   A robot moves on the 4 × 4 square grid shown below.
    A subroutine, SqMove, is part of a flow diagram that tells the robot how to move.

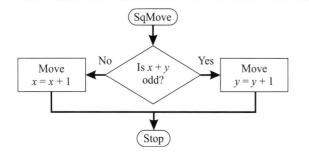

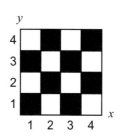

Draw a flow diagram to show how the robot moves. The flow diagram should:
   • Ask the user to enter which square the robot starts on.
   • Use the subroutine SqMove.
   • Stop when the robot reaches the top or the right of the grid.

This is when x = 4 or y = 4

[Total 6 marks]

6   A garden centre is having a sale. New customers get £5 off for items costing £50 or more.
    Existing customers get a discount based on the stock level of the item, as shown below.

Stock Level	0 – 9	10 – 99	100 +
Price Reduction	0 %	10 %	20 %

a) Draw a flow diagram to calculate the cost of an item using the information above.

[6]

b) A wheelbarrow costs £100 and 110 are in stock.
   Use your flow diagram to find how much one wheelbarrow would cost an existing customer.

£ ....
[1]

[Total 7 marks]

Exam Practice Tip

Unless a question says otherwise, when asked to write an algorithm you have the option of using pseudocode or a flow diagram. Don't get too caught up on the wording of your algorithm but make sure that it is clear and easy to interpret.

Section Four — Algorithms

44

Search Algorithms

1   Nicola has a list of numbers: 2, 3, 7, 5, 13, 11.

   a) She says, "I can't use a binary search to find 13." Why is this the case?

   ....
   [1]

   b) Show the steps of a linear search to find 13 in the list above.

   [2]
   [Total 3 marks]

2   Sonia has a sorted list of ice cream flavours that she sells in her shop.

   a) Show the stages of a binary search to find the word 'butterscotch' in the list below.

butterscotch	chocolate	mint	strawberry	vanilla

   [4]

   b) Give **one** advantage of using a binary search over a linear search.

   ....
   ....
   [1]

   c) Six more flavours are added to Sonia's list. The list is still in alphabetical order.
      Explain why it would only take two iterations of a binary search to find the ninth item in the list.

   ....
   ....
   ....
   ....
   [3]
   [Total 8 marks]

Sorting Algorithms

1 Use the insertion sort algorithm to put these European cities into alphabetical order.

Riga	Paris	Oslo	Baku	Minsk

[Total 4 marks]

2 Six athletes compete in a long jump competition. Their best jumps are shown below.

5.32 m	5.50 m	5.39 m	6.50 m	6.28 m	6.14 m

Show the stages of a bubble sort to list these jumps in order from shortest to longest.

[Total 4 marks]

3 Kim has a hand of playing cards, all of the same suit: 3, 7, 6, 2, 5.

a) Arrange the cards in order from highest to lowest using:

   i) An insertion sort.   ii) A merge sort.

[4]   *[4]*

b) Explain **one** benefit of using an insertion sort over a merge sort on a computer.

....

....

[2]

[Total 10 marks]

4 A musician is sorting his CD collection by year released, from oldest to newest.

A sample of the sorted list is shown below.

1989	1990	1992	1998	2000

a) Show all the comparisons of a bubble sort algorithm to show that the list above is already in order.

[2]

b) By looking at the number of comparisons, explain why a bubble sort is useful for checking if a list is ordered.

....

....

[2]

[Total 4 marks]

5 The list below shows the calorie content of different packets of sweets.

450	350	230	180	650	500	340	270

a) Show the stages of a merge sort to arrange the list from lowest to highest.

[4]

b) Give a reason why the merge sort:

i) Splits the list into single items.

....

[1]

ii) Uses ordered lists at each merging step.

....

[1]

[Total 6 marks]

Exam Practice Tip

Sorting algorithms can be lengthy, but don't miss out any steps — make sure you show **every** stage of the algorithm in the exam. This way the examiner knows you clearly understand the algorithm and can reward you some easy marks.

Mixed Questions

1   Mike is posting an online advert on a forum to promote his band's upcoming tour.

a) Outline **one** decomposition and a matching abstraction process when creating the advert.

Decomposition: ....

....

Abstraction: ....

....

[2]

b) The algorithm on the right shows how the cost (in £) of an advert for basic and premium forum users is calculated.

What is the difference in cost between a basic and a premium user?

```
STRING user
REAL cost = 5.0
user = INPUT("Premium or basic?")
IF user == "premium" THEN
    cost = cost * 0.5
ELSE
    cost = cost + 1.0
ENDIF
print(cost)
```

£........................

[2]

[Total 4 marks]

2   Every 5 minutes, an app on a mobile phone records the electrical current (in mA) passing through a pair of connected headphones.

A sample of the readings is shown below.

10 mA	15 mA	12 mA	18 mA	20 mA

a) Show the stages of a linear search to find the value '12 mA' in the list above.

[2]

b) If a reading is greater than 30 mA the mobile phone will buzz and then the program will stop.
If not, the program will wait 5 minutes before taking another reading.
Draw a flow diagram to show this program.

Your flow diagram should show an iteration — a loop that repeats the task.

[6]

[Total 8 marks]

3 Leigh has a list of six gymnastics apparatus.

Floor	Pommel	Rings	Vault	Parallel Bars	High Bar

a) Show the stages of a merge sort to list the apparatus into alphabetical order.

[4]

b) Show the stages of a binary search to find 'Rings' from your ordered list above.

[4]

[Total 8 marks]

4 Mr Spencer is playing a board game which uses two 4-sided dice. The table shows what a player will score depending on which numbers the two dice land on. * means have another roll.

		Dice 1			
		1	**2**	**3**	**4**
Dice 2	**1**	0	*	0	*
	2	*	4	*	6
	3	0	*	0	*
	4	*	6	*	8

Use this table to work out the rules for scoring — look at how odd and even dice rolls affect the scores.

a) Draw a flow diagram to show how to **play** and **score** this game.

[6]

b) Each score is stored in a list. At the end of the game the list is searched to see if an 8 was scored. Tick the most suitable search algorithm for this task and explain your answer.

Binary Search ☐   Linear Search ☐

....

[2]

[Total 8 marks]

Section Four — Algorithms

Programming Basics

Warm-Up

Circle the items that would be best represented using an integer data type:

The nickname of your best friend.

The weight of one potato in kg.

The number on a rolled dice.

An email address.

The number of people on a football pitch.

The age of a pet in whole months.

The length of a car to the nearest metre.

---

1   A bakery stores data about the pies it makes.

Complete the table below by giving the most appropriate data type for each bit of information.

Information	Example	Data Type
Flavour	Apple and Strawberry	
Weight (kg)	1.35	
Quantity in stock	7	
Gluten-free?	False	

[Total 4 marks]

---

2   State what the code will do in each of the following:

a) `int("76423")`

....
[1]

b) `ASC("T")`

....
[1]

c) `12 MOD 5`

....
[1]

[Total 3 marks]

---

3   A pedestrian crossing uses a button to request the traffic to stop. State the data type that you would use to record each of these variables and give a reason for your answer.

a) A variable to record whether the button has been pressed or not.

Data type: ....

Reason: ....
[2]

b) A variable to record how many whole seconds it's been since the button was pressed.

Data type: ....

Reason: ....
[2]

[Total 4 marks]

4   A teacher writes the following program to analyse
     the test scores of a pupil. Line 03 is missing.

```
01  x = INPUT("Enter mark for test 1")
02  y = INPUT("Enter mark for test 2")
03
04  print(z)
```

Complete line 03 so that the program:

a) Calculates the total score of the pupil.

....
                                                                                                                    [1]

b) Calculates if their score in test 1 is greater than or equal to the score on test 2.

....
                                                                                                                    [1]

c) Calculates the pupil's combined score from both tests as a percentage out of 160 marks available.

> To find the percentage, divide the total
> marks the pupil got by the total number
> of marks available and multiply by 100.

....
                                                                                                                    [1]
                                                                                                  [Total 3 marks]

5   A petrol station needs a program to calculate the cost of fuel for each customer.

a) Identify appropriate data types for:

   i)   The name of the fuel that the customer used.

....
                                                                                                                    [1]

   ii) The total cost of the customers fuel.

....
                                                                                                                    [1]

b) Explain why it's important to use the correct data type to store information.

....

....

....
                                                                                                                    [2]

c) Describe with an example how the function str() might be used when printing the receipt.

....

....

....
                                                                                                                    [2]
                                                                                                  [Total 6 marks]

Exam Practice Tip

Questions about data types are usually a great way to pick up a few easy marks in your exam, so it's really important
that you know the names of the different data types and the best situation to use each one. As for the different
operators — they'll crop up all the way through your exam so commit them to memory now so you don't come unstuck.

Constants and Variables

1 The program below calculates the cost of a burger in pounds at a fast food restaurant.
A standard burger costs £6.50 with additional costs for toppings and eating in the restaurant.

```
CONST standard = 6.5
INT toppings = 0
BOOL eat_in = false
toppings = INPUT("How many toppings?")
eat_in = INPUT("Are they eating in?")
IF eat_in == true THEN
    print(standard + 0.5*toppings + 1)
ELSE
    print(standard + 0.5*toppings)
ENDIF
```

a) List **all** the variables in this program.

....
[2]

b) How much extra does it cost to eat your burger inside the restaurant?

....
[1]

c) The restaurant manager says that 0.5 should have been declared as a constant.
Give **two** reasons for declaring this value as a constant.

1 ....

2 ....
[2]

[Total 5 marks]

2 The program below calculates the value of an investment at the end of one year.

```
CONST investment as REAL
VAR rate as REAL
VAR interest as INT
INPUT investment
INPUT rate
FOR x = 1 to 12
    interest = rate * investment
    investment = investment + interest
NEXT x
print(investment)
```

Identify **two** problems with the program.

1 ....

....

2 ....

....
[Total 2 marks]

3 Jeremiah is writing a program for a gym where customers need to scan their
gym card to get in and out. The program should keep track of how many
people are in the gym and refuse entry once the gym is at maximum capacity.

Describe **one** constant and **two** variables that the program could use.
For each one explain why it should be a constant or variable.

Constant ....

....

Variable 1 ....

....

Variable 2 ....

....
[Total 6 marks]

Strings

Given that `fish = "lobster"`, draw lines to match each of these string methods with the correct output.

fish.length	bst
fish.subString(0, 3)	7
fish.upper	LOBSTER
fish.subString(2, 3)	lob

1 A digital radio stores the current date as a string under the variable name `date`. The radio is broken and is stuck on the date: 8 January 2016

State the output from each of the following pieces of code:

a) `date.length`

....
[1]

b) `date.subString[0] + date.subString(10,4)`

....
[1]

c) `date.subString(2,3).upper`

....
[1]

[Total 3 marks]

2 A juice company generates a product ID for each of its fruit juices. The product ID is generated using string concatenation on the first three letters of the fruit (in uppercase) and the volume of fruit juice in ml. E.g. a 500 ml carton of apple juice would be APP500.

a) Define what is meant by string concatenation.

....
[1]

b) What would the product code be for a 2000 ml carton of orange juice?

....
[1]

c) Complete the algorithm below so that line 05 reassigns the uppercase name of the fruit to the `fruit` variable and line 06 assigns the final product ID to the `prodID` variable.

```
01 STRING fruit, prodID
02 INT volume
03 fruit = INPUT("Enter the name of the fruit.")
04 volume = INPUT("Enter the volume of the juice.")

05 fruit = ....................................................................

06 prodID = ..................................................................
07 print(prodID)
```
[3]

[Total 5 Marks]

Program Flow

Put each of these statements into the correct box below.

REPEAT-UNTIL   IF-THEN-ELSE   SWITCH-CASE   DO-UNTIL   IF-ELSEIF   WHILE

Selection Statements	Iteration Statements

1 Jasminda has written the following program to convert minutes into hours and minutes.

```
INT minutes, hours, mins
minutes = INPUT("Enter a number of minutes")
hours = minutes DIV 60
mins = minutes MOD 60
print(str(hours) + " hours and " + str(mins) + " minutes")
```

a) Is this an example of a sequence, selection or iteration? Tick the correct box.

Sequence ☐   Selection ☐   Iteration ☐

[1]

b) What would the program print if the input was 150?

....

[1]

[Total 2 marks]

2 An electric heater has four temperature settings (0, 1, 2 and 3).
The code below controls the temperature of the heater.

```
INT setting, temperature
SWITCH setting:
    CASE 3:
        temperature = 50
    CASE 2:
        temperature = 30
    CASE 1:
        temperature = 20
    CASE 0:
        temperature = 0
ENDSWITCH
```

a) Rewrite this program using a different selection statement.

An ELSEIF statement will help you check lots of conditions.

[3]

b) Give **two** reasons why a switch-case statement is appropriate for this program.

1 ....

2 ....

[2]

[Total 5 marks]

Section Five — Programming

54

3 Salik needs a program that will ask users to create a password and then check if the password contains at least six characters. If it contains fewer than six characters the user must try again, otherwise the user is informed that their password is valid.

a) Write an appropriate program for Salik.

VAR password as ....

DO

    password = ...("Please enter a password")

UNTIL ....

print(...)

[4]

b) Give **one** reason why a programmer might want to use a do-until loop instead of a while loop.

....

....

[1]

[Total 5 marks]

4 In a basketball arcade game a player gets 10 shots to score as many baskets as they can. The program on the right keeps track of a player's score.

```
INT score = 0
BOOL basket
FOR x = 1 to 10
    Player shoots
    Update basket
    IF basket = true
        score = score + 1
    ENDIF
NEXT x
output(score)
```

a) What are the possible values for the variable basket?

....

[1]

b) Explain why a count-controlled loop has been used instead of a condition-controlled loop.

....

....

[2]

c) Describe how you would adapt the program so that a player could specify the amount of shots that they want to take.

....

....

[2]

d) Another basketball game gives the player an unlimited amount of shots until they've scored 5 baskets. Explain why a condition-controlled loop would be more appropriate for this game.

....

....

[2]

[Total 7 marks]

5 Joanne wants a program that will print a sentence she has typed once the sentence is finished. The sentence will be finished when Joanne types a full stop, question mark or exclamation mark (".", "?" or "!").

Use the variables `keypress` and `sentence` to write a suitable program for Joanne.

Use 'Input keypress' to mean wait for a key to be pressed and assign the value to the keypress variable.

[Total 5 marks]

6 Karl and John are playing snap. Write an algorithm that:
- Asks for the name of the winner of each game.
- After ten games checks who has won more and displays the winner's name or tells them that it's a draw.

You'll need variables to keep track of the winner of each game and the number of games each player has won.

[Total 6 marks]

Exam Practice Tip

When it comes to writing programs and algorithms in the exam it's important that you remember to lay them out correctly — this means declaring variables before they are used, using indentation and finishing statements, e.g. with ENDIF or ENDSWITCH. Another key thing to remember is to use == when you mean "is equal to" and = as the assignment operator — it may sound simple but if you get it wrong you could lose a mark or two in the exam.

Boolean Operators

Circle all of the Boolean expressions that are true.

12 > 4 AND 5 == 5   12 <= 4 OR 10 != 5   7 >= 3 AND 91 > 99

NOT(11 == 3)   9 == 8 OR 2 > 16   NOT(9 > 4 AND 5 < 2)

1   A garden centre has a climate monitoring system that gives warnings if the temperature and humidity aren't at suitable levels. The climate monitoring system contains this algorithm.

```
IF humidity == 50 AND (temperature > 16 AND temperature < 25) THEN
    print("Humidity and temperature at acceptable levels.")
ELSEIF temperature <= 16 OR temperature >= 25 THEN
    print("Warning — Please alter the temperature.")
ELSE
    print("Warning — Please alter the humidity.")
ENDIF
```

a) What will the output be if humidity = 30 and temperature = 16?

....

[1]

b) What will the output be if humidity = 30 and temperature = 20?

....

[1]

[Total 2 marks]

2   A car park barrier will only open if the driver inserts a paid ticket or a valid permit. Write an algorithm using the boolean variables barrierUp, ticketPaid and permitValid that will check the status of a driver's ticket or permit before opening the barrier.

[Total 3 marks]

3   A tumble dryer will only be allowed to start if all of the following conditions are met:
   • the real variable weight is more than 1.5 and less than 15.0
   • the boolean variable doorClosed is true.

Write an algorithm that checks these conditions before allowing the tumble dryer to start.

[Total 3 marks]

File Handling

1 Frances has written a list of jobs she has to do and stored it in the ToDoList.txt file shown on the right.

> 1. Clean my room.
> 2. Computer Science homework.
> 3. Organise my stamp collection.

a) Describe what each line of the code below does.

```
01 myList = openRead("ToDoList.txt")
02 print(myList.readLine())
03 myList.close()
```

Line 01 ....

Line 02 ....

Line 03 ....

[3]

Frances writes the following code to add an extra job to the bottom of her list.

```
myList = openWrite("ToDoList.txt")
myList.writeLine("4. Make lunch for parents.")
myList.close()
```

b) Explain why the code Frances has written will not work as intended.

....

....

....

[2]

[Total 5 marks]

2 Omar has written an adventure story in the file adventure.txt.

Write an algorithm that allows a user to print Omar's adventure story one line at a time.
- Each time the user presses the "y" key the next line of the story should be printed.
- The algorithm should end when it's at the end of the text file.

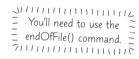
You'll need to use the endOfFile() command.

[Total 5 marks]

Storing Data

1   Harry wants to create a database to store information about the animals at his local zoo.

Complete the table below to show the most suitable data type for each field of Harry's database.

Field	Example	Data Type
Animal_type	Giraffe	
Number_of_animals	5	
Average_weight	1200.2	
Continent_of_origin	Africa	
Meat_eater	True	

[Total 5 marks]

2   The cars table below shows some data on the used cars that a car dealership has in stock.

CarID	Registration	Make	Type	Price	Engine_size
1	NF09 APY	Stanton	Hatchback	2500	1.4
2	SZ15 LUY	Fenwick	Saloon	4800	1.8
3	FQ55 ALW	Stanton	Hatchback	1700	2.1
4	SQ57 TTW	Fenwick	Estate	2300	2.8
5	NZ12 MBE	Stanton	Saloon	5200	1.8

a) How many records does this table have?

....

[1]

b) Explain the difference between a record and a field.

....

....

....

[2]

c) Draw tables showing what would be returned by each of the following SQL commands:

     i)   SELECT Registration, Make FROM cars WHERE Price < 2500

Registration	Make
....	....
....	....

[2]

     ii)   SELECT Make, Type FROM cars WHERE Registration LIKE "N%"

[2]

[Total 7 marks]

3 Some of the records in a school's database are shown in the `classes` table on the right. It stores the surname, year group and form of every pupil in the school.

Surname	Year Group	Form
Simpson	10	A
Gleeson	11	C
Kane	9	B
Stoodley	11	C
Lewis	10	A
Simpson	10	A

a) Identify one problem with this database table.

....
[1]

b) Give **two** reasons why it is useful to store pupil data in records.

1 ....

2 ....
[2]

c) Describe what the following SQL query will return.
   `SELECT * FROM classes WHERE Year Group = 10`

....

....
[2]

[Total 5 marks]

4 A comic book store keeps information about each of its comics in a database. The table below shows the first two entries from the `comics` table.

ID Number	Title	Publication date	Length	Genre	Rating
0001	Hike of hope	04-05-2015	82	Adventure	5
0002	Voyage of Destiny	05-09-2015	65	Science Fiction	4

a) i) Identify a suitable field in the table above to use as a primary key.

....
[1]

   ii) Explain why database tables use primary keys.

....

....
[2]

b) Write an SQL query to return:
   i) the titles of all Science Fiction comics.

....
[2]

   ii) the titles and lengths of all the comics that have fewer than 50 pages and a rating of 3.

....
[2]

   iii) all the fields for comics with titles that begin with the letter H.

....
[2]

[Total 9 marks]

Section Five — Programming

Arrays

1   The top 5 high scores in an arcade game are stored in the highscores array shown below.

	0	1	2	3	4
Score	510 000	453 000	442 000	440 500	429 000

a) State the output if this code is run: print(highscores[3])

....

[1]

b) State the output if this code is run: print(highscores[0] - highscores[4])

....

[1]

c) A player's score is temporarily stored as the integer variable newScore.
   Write an algorithm to check whether the highscores array should be updated or not.

   IF .... THEN

       Update the array.

   ENDIF

[2]

[Total 4 marks]

2   Kerry owns a cupcake shop which sells the following flavours of cupcake:

   Vanilla   Banana   Strawberry   Cherry   Caramel

a) Write some code that will create a one-dimensional array called cupcakes
   which displays this list of cupcakes in the order they appear above.

> Remember to declare the
> array before assigning
> values to each position.

[3]

b) Write a line of code to output the first item in the list.

....

[1]

c) Kerry wants to change the cherry cupcake for a raspberry one. Write a line of code to do this.

....

[1]

[Total 5 marks]

3   A 2D array is used to store the names of the top 3 pupils in each event of a sports day.

a) What data type should each element of the array be assigned?

....

[1]

b) Give **three** reasons for using a 2D array to store this data.

1 ....

2 ....

3 ....

[3]

[Total 4 marks]

4   John and three of his friends are training to run a marathon. John records how many miles he and three friends ran each day last week. John stores the data in a 2D array called `distanceRun`.

		0	1	2	3	4	5	6
		Days of the week						
Runner	**0**	9	10	8	12	0	6	9
	1	10	12	15	15	0	0	10
	2	15	14	13	16	0	8	9
	3	6	8	9	10	12	12	0

The distance run on day 0 by runner 2 is given by `distanceRun[0, 2]`.

a) Write the code to display the distance run on day 4 by runner 3.

....

[1]

b) Write an algorithm that takes a runner number as an input and
outputs the total number of miles that they ran over the week.

[4]

c) John has written the function `milesConvert()` which takes a distance in miles
and returns the equivalent distance in km. E.g. `milesConvert(5)` would return 8.
Write an algorithm to convert all distances in the array to km.

[3]

[Total 8 marks]

Section Five — Programming

Sub Programs

1 Write a function that takes an integer as a parameter and returns the difference between the integer's cube and it's square.

[Total 3 marks]

2 Isabel is developing a stopwatch application to be used on her smartphone.

a) Give **three** benefits that sub programs will bring to Isabel's application.

1 ....

2 ....

3 ....

[3]

b) Give **one** difference between a function and a procedure.

....

[1]

[Total 4 marks]

3 The function roll(n) simulates the outcome of one random roll of an n-sided dice. E.g. roll(6) will randomly return either 1, 2, 3, 4, 5 or 6.

a) Noel has declared a local variable inside the function.
Explain **two** differences between local variables and global variables.

1 ....

....

2 ....

....

[4]

b) Noel wants to use his function in a dice game where two identical dice are rolled together.
   • The player can choose the number of sides that the dice have.
   • The player's score is the number of rolls it takes until both dice land on the same number.
   Write a sub program that takes the number of sides of
   the dice as a parameter and outputs a player's score.

[5]

[Total 9 marks]

4 Lenny is writing a program for an exercise bike that adjusts the difficulty depending on information about the user.

a) One of Lenny's sub programs takes `weight` as a parameter.

   i) Define what is meant by a parameter.

      ....

      [1]

   ii) What is the scope of a parameter?

      ....

      [1]

   iii) Outline how arguments are different from parameters.

      ....

      [1]

b) The code on the right appears near the start of Lenny's program.

   i) Explain what the first line of this code does.

```
global difficulty as INT
INPUT weight
PROCEDURE setInitialDifficulty(weight as INT)
    difficulty = weight DIV 6
ENDPROCEDURE
```

      ....

      ....

      [2]

   ii) Describe what the `setInitialDifficulty` procedure does.

      ....

      ....

      [2]

c) Lenny wants a sub program that adjusts the difficulty depending on the user's heart rate.

   • If their heart rate is below 90 then the difficulty level should be increased by 1.

   • If their heart rate is over 140 then the difficulty level should be decreased by 1.

   • If their heart rate is over 160 then the difficulty level should be set to 0 and the warning message "Slow Down!" should appear.

Write a sub program that takes heart rate as a parameter and adjusts the difficulty level as stated above.

[4]

[Total 11 marks]

Exam Practice Tip

A good way to approach "Write a sub program to..." questions is by writing down the parameters you want to put in and the values you want to get out of the sub program. If you simply want to carry out a set of step-by-step instructions then a procedure is the sub program for you, but if you want to return a value then you'll need a function.

Mixed Questions

1 A microwave has three settings to control its power output:
Defrost (200W), Medium (650W) or High (900W). The name of the
setting and power output are shown on the microwave's digital display.

a) Complete the table showing what data type should be used to store these variables.

Variable	Example	Data Type
setting	Defrost	
power	200	

[2]

b) Write a program that checks the setting variable, then changes the power output
and updates the setting and power on the digital display.

The digital display shows e.g "Defrost 200W".

[4]

[Total 6 marks]

2 A sat nav uses the following sub program to calculate
the average speed of a car during a journey.

```
FUNCTION averageSpeed(distance as REAL, time as REAL) as REAL
    IF distance > 0 AND time > 0 THEN
        return(distance / time)
    ELSE
        return(0.0)
    ENDIF
ENDFUNCTION
```

a) What value will be returned from averageSpeed(110.0, 2.0)?

....

[1]

b) The one dimensional array, speeds, stores the average speeds of the last 10 journeys,
with the most recent journey being stored in position 0. Write a sub program that takes
the average speed from a new journey as a parameter and updates the journeySpeeds array.

Update the last element of the array first to avoid losing data.

[4]

[Total 5 marks]

3 The Prime Koalas are a band consisting of four members:
John on guitar, Paul on bass, Cheryl on vocals and Ida on drums.

a) Complete the code below to generate a 2D array containing
the names and instruments of all the band members.

```
ARRAY primeKoalas[4, 2]
primeKoalas[0, 0] = "John"
primeKoalas[1, 0] = "Paul"
primeKoalas[2, 0] = "Cheryl"
primeKoalas[3, 0] = "Ida"
```

[2]

b) John wants to open the empty text file called musicians.txt and write to it.
Each line of the file should contain a different band member and their instrument.
Write an algorithm that uses your array in part a) to write this information to the text file.

[3]

c) Explain **two** advantages of storing data in a text file instead of in an array.

1 ....

....

2 ....

....

[4]

d) The sub program toSpeech() takes a string as a parameter, turns the string into audio data and
reads it out loud. Write a procedure using toSpeech() that takes a file name as a parameter
and reads out all the data in the file.

[5]

[Total 14 marks]

Section Five — Programming

Defensive Design

1   A retailer keeps a database of its loyalty card holders. The retailer stores the following data for each loyalty card holder: name, age, postcode and customer number.

Name	Age	Postcode	Customer No.
Carol Foreman	20	NE85 3TW	100278
Peter Taylor	55	HA55 8PZ	223327

a) Define the term input validation.

....

[1]

b) Give **two** suitable input validation checks for an entry in the age field.

Think about the type of data values that each field should take.

1 ....

2 ....

[2]

c) Give **two** suitable input validation checks for an entry in the postcode field.

1 ....

2 ....

[2]

[Total 5 marks]

2   Jessica has written the program below to calculate the area of any triangle with a base length less than 20.

```
REAL num1
INT num2
INT num3
num2 = INPUT("Enter a base length")
num3 = INPUT("Enter a height")
IF num2 < 20 THEN
num1 = (num2 * num3) / 2
print(num1)
ELSE
print("Base length too long.")
ENDIF
```

Describe with an example how Jessica can use each of the following to improve the maintainability of her code.

Indentation ....

....

Comments ....

....

Variable names ....

....

[Total 6 marks]

3 Jane uses authentication in her program, which manages a hospital's patient records.

a) Define the term authentication.

....
[1]

b) Explain why Jane might want to use multiple layers of authentication in her program.

....

....
[2]

c) Identify **one** disadvantage of using authentication in a program.

....
[1]
[Total 4 marks]

4 Malcolm leads a team of developers writing an air traffic control program.

a) The team agree some defensive design conventions before they start programming.
Explain **two** conventions that could improve the maintainability of the program.

1 ....

....

2 ....

....
[4]

b) Malcolm wants to prevent users from putting spaces in the flight numbers.
Give an example of how he can do this using defensive design.

....

....
[2]
[Total 6 marks]

5 A website's payment form requires users to input their credit card details.
E.g. name, card number, expiration date, security code, etc.

Evaluate the impact of only using input validation to check the details.

....

....

....

....

....

....
[Total 6 marks]

Testing

1   Huey is designing a smartphone app. His code is currently full of syntax errors and logic errors.

a) State what is meant by a syntax error.

....
[1]

b) Describe what would happen when the code is translated if all the syntax errors were corrected but the logic errors were left unchanged.

....

....
[2]

[Total 3 marks]

2   Tiffany writes some code to check if an entered pincode is between 4 and 6 characters long.

```
STRING pincode
INPUT pincode
IF pincode.length >= 4 OR pincode.length <= 6 THEN
    print("Valid pincode"
ELSE
    print("Not a valid pincode, please try again")
ENDIF
```

a) Identify the syntax error in Tiffany's code and suggest how she could correct it.

Error ....

Correction ....
[2]

b) Identify the logic error in Tiffany's code and suggest how she could correct it.

Error ....

Correction ....
[2]

[Total 4 marks]

3 A holiday company has written a simple program to calculate the price of its group holiday packages. The program asks the user to input the group size — if the group size is smaller than two or greater than 10 the program displays an error message. If not, the price (in £s) is calculated by multiplying the group size by 50 and then adding 10.

a) Describe how the company can use a test plan to check for logic errors in the program.

....

....

....

[3]

b) Complete the test plan below by filling in the missing spaces.

Test Data	Expected Outcome	Reasons for test
Group_Size = 4		
	460	
Group_Size = 12		Check what happens if input too large.

[5]

[Total 8 marks]

4 Jackson is developing a program to monitor the speed at which athletes in a marathon are running.

a) Jackson would like to test his program. Define the following terms:

i) Final testing

....

....

[2]

ii) Iterative testing

....

....

[2]

b) Explain **one** advantage and **one** disadvantage of using final testing.

Advantage ....

....

Disadvantage ....

....

[4]

[Total 8 marks]

Section Six — Design, Testing and IDEs

Translators

1 Jeffrey has written a flight simulation game in a high-level language.

Identify **two** types of translator that can turn high-level languages into machine code, and describe the translation process for each one.

Translator 1 ....

....

Translator 2 ....

....

[Total 4 marks]

2 A company specialises in writing programs using low-level languages.

a) Identify **two** reasons why some programmers still use low-level languages.

1 ....

2 ....

[2]

b) Explain why programmers might prefer to use an assembly language over machine code.

....

....

[2]

c) State the type of translator used to translate assembly languages into machine code.

....

[1]

[Total 5 marks]

3 Cleo is writing a program to find suitable recipes based on selected ingredients. Cleo has used a high-level programming language.

Describe **three** differences between high-level languages and low-level languages.

1 ....

....

2 ....

....

3 ....

....

[Total 6 marks]

Section Six — Design, Testing and IDEs

Integrated Development Environments

Below is a sketch of the layout of a new Integrated Development Environment (IDE). In each box, briefly describe the purpose of that feature.

Code Editor	Breakpoints
Error Diagnostics	

1 Cynthia is writing code for a tablet computer application aimed at children.

a) Explain how each of the following tools in the Integrated Development Environment (IDE) could help Cynthia write her application.

Translator ....

....

Error Diagnostics ....

....

Code editor ....

....

[6]

b) Cynthia's code contains syntax errors. Outline a process that could be used to correct the syntax errors using all of the IDE tools mentioned in part a).

....

....

....

[3]

[Total 9 marks]

2 Max is writing some complex software for interactive guides in a museum. His program is producing logic errors, and he is having trouble finding where they occur.

Explain how Max can use Integrated Development Environment tools to find the logic errors.

....

....

....

....

[Total 4 marks]

Mixed Questions

1   Tony is writing a program for a dice game. A player starts with a score of 0 and rolls a six-sided dice as many times as they want. After each roll they add the number the dice lands on to their score. The aim is to get as close to 21 as possible. If you go over 21 you get a score of 0.

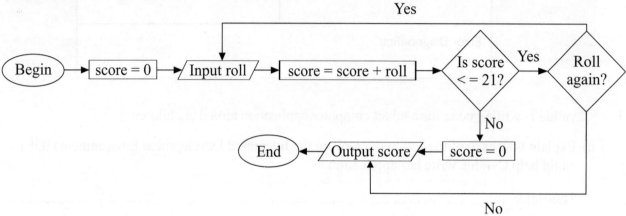

    a) Tony designs a test plan for his game.
       Explain why it's important for the test plan to include erroneous test data.

       ....

       ....

       [2]

    b) Tony tests each of the following values for the dice rolls. State the type of test data, the expected outcome and the actual outcome of each test.

       i)   5, 6, 4, 3, 2

          Type of data ....

          Expected Outcome ....

          Actual Outcome ....

          [3]

       ii)   5, 9, 3, 2

          Type of data ....

          Think about what input data
          Tony's program should accept.

          Expected Outcome ....

          Actual Outcome ....

          [3]

    c) Identify **two** ways that Tony could use input validation in his dice game.

       1 ....

       2 ....

       [2]

       [Total 10 marks]

2 Natasha has written some code in a high-level language, which checks whether the email address the user inputs contains an "@" symbol.

```
FUNCTION checkEmail(email as STRING) as BOOL
    BOOL valid = FALSE
    FOR x = 0 to 10
        IF email[x] = "@" THEN
            valid = TRUE
        ENDIF
    NEXT x
    RETURN valid
ENDFUNCTION
```

a) State **one** logic error in Natasha's code and explain why it is a logic error.

Logic error ....

Explanation ....

[2]

b) Explain **one** way Natasha could improve the maintainability of her program.

....

....

[2]

c) Explain **one** other way that Natasha could use input validation to check email addresses.

Think about other features that all email addresses contain.

....

....

[2]

d) Natasha needs to translate her program into machine code. Outline **two** differences in the way a compiler and interpreter would translate her program.

1 ....

....

2 ....

....

[4]

[Total 10 marks]

3 An exam board is developing automated software to calculate students' final exam grades.

Evaluate the extent to which the different features of an IDE can help the exam board to develop a well-maintained program.

....

....

....

....

....

....

[Total 6 marks]

Section Six — Design, Testing and IDEs

Logic

1   Two truth tables are given below. A and B are inputs. P and Q are outputs.

Draw the correct logic gates for each of these truth tables.

a)

A	P
0	1
1	0

b)

A	B	Q
0	0	0
0	1	1
1	0	1
1	1	1

[1]

[1]

[Total 2 marks]

2   A logic gate can be written as P = A AND B.

a) State the value of input B when input A is 1 and output P is 0.

B = ...
[1]

b) A NOT logic gate is placed after the AND logic gate to make the logic diagram below.
State the input values when output P is 0.

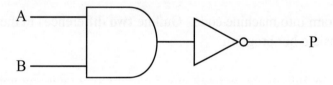

A = ... B = ...
[1]

[Total 2 marks]

3   Ollie writes a truth table for the logic circuit Q = A OR (NOT B).

a) Complete his truth table below.

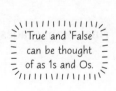
'True' and 'False' can be thought of as 1s and 0s.

A	B	Q
FALSE	FALSE	TRUE
FALSE	TRUE	
	FALSE	
TRUE		

[3]

b) Ollie draws the following logic diagram for Q = A OR (NOT B).
Annotate the diagram to show **two** things that are incorrect.

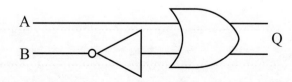

[2]

[Total 5 marks]

4   A series of transistors make the two-level logic circuit (NOT A) AND (B AND C).

a) Complete the truth table below.

A	B	C	NOT A	B AND C	(NOT A) AND (B AND C)
0	0	0			
0	0	1			
0	1	0			
0	1	1			
1	0	0			
1	0	1			
1	1	0			
1	1	1			

[3]

b) Draw the logic diagram that represents (NOT A) AND (B AND C).

[3]

[Total 6 marks]

5   A car uses a logic circuit to decide whether to start the engine or not.
   • The car has two buttons, labelled **S** (START) and **D** (DRIVE).
     If both buttons are on, the engine will start.
   • The engine also starts if the ignition switch **I** is turned on.

a) Draw the logic circuit diagram for this system, with **Z** as an output.

[3]

b) Write a Boolean expression for this logic circuit.

....
[1]

c) State all possible values of the inputs and outputs if:
   i)   Button D is on but the car doesn't start.

....
[1]

   ii) Buttons I and S are both on.

....

....
[2]

[Total 7 marks]

Units

1   Misha wants to save some music files onto a solid state drive (SSD).

a) State which SSD has the largest capacity:
   250 gigabyte (GB), 200 000 megabyte (MB) or 0.3 terabyte (TB).

....

[1]

b) Calculate how many 5 MB music files Misha could save onto a 250 GB SSD.

....

[2]

[Total 3 marks]

2   Computers process data in binary code and often use check digits.

a) Outline what is meant by a check digit.

....

....

[2]

b) Describe how binary is used to represent data in computers.

....

....

[2]

c) An even parity bit has been added to the end of three 7-bit binary codes to create
   the 8-bit binary codes below. Identify and explain which code contains an error.

Code 1	Code 2	Code 3
10101011	10100101	10010011

....

....

[2]

d) Explain how a binary code containing a parity bit can be
   read incorrectly without any errors being detected.

....

....

[2]

[Total 8 marks]

Binary Numbers

Black dots on the first binary clock below indicate the time 11:17:59.
Shade the dots on the second clock to show the time 15:57:40.

1   Work out these conversions.

a) Convert the 8-bit binary number 10010011 into a denary number.

....
[1]

b) Convert the denary number 252 into an 8-bit binary number.

....
[1]

[Total 2 marks]

2   An 8-bit binary addition involves adding two 8-bit numbers and getting an 8-bit answer.

a) Add the binary numbers 00111001 and 01010110.

....
[2]

b) Computers can encounter overflow when adding binary numbers.
   i)   Give an example of an 8-bit binary addition where an overflow occurs.

[2]

   ii) Explain how a computer deals with the overflow.

....

....
[2]

[Total 6 marks]

Section Seven — Data Representation

3 Binary shifts can be used to quickly multiply and divide binary numbers.

a) Complete a 3 place left shift on the binary number 00011010.

....

[1]

b) State an appropriate binary shift to divide a binary number by 4 and use it on 11010100.

....

[2]

c) Yasha says "Adding a binary number to itself is the same as a 2 place left shift."
Is he correct? Explain your answer.

....

....

[2]

[Total 5 marks]

4 In a video game, every 8-bit binary number represents a unique magic word or a spell.
The last digit determines if it is a magic word (0) or a spell (1).

a) State how many unique magic words there are.

....

[1]

Spells are made by adding the binary numbers of words together and then adding 00000001.
Overflow bits are ignored. A sample of spells and words are shown below.

Number	Word
00110100	Shazam
01010000	Abra
01100110	Kadabra
10011100	Hocus
11001010	Pocus

Number	Spell
00100011	Teleport
01101111	Fireball
10110111	Blizzard
11110001	Zap
11111111	Earthquake

Because the last digit is always 0, this is the same as changing the last digit from a 0 to a 1.

b) What spell is made with the words 'Abra' and 'Kadabra'?

....

[2]

c) Identify **two** words from the table that could have been used to make the Earthquake spell.

.... and ....

[2]

[Total 5 marks]

Exam Practice Tip

If you end up with too many bits after some 8-bit binary arithmetic and don't know what to do you could be giving away some easy marks! Make sure you use the technical term for this, **overflow**, and can explain it clearly.

Hexadecimal Numbers

Fill in the boxes below to complete the hexadecimal equations.

A + ☐ = C   6 + ☐ = E   ☐ + 6 = C   F + ☐ = 1E

1 Work out these hexadecimal problems.

Remember — no calculators allowed.

a) What is the largest denary number that can be made using 2 hex characters?

....
[1]

b) Convert the hexadecimal number 37 into denary.

....
[2]

c) Convert the denary number 45 into hexadecimal.

....
[2]
[Total 5 marks]

2 A security program encrypts passwords using a hexadecimal conversion.

The binary code of each letter for the password 'CAT' is shown below.

01000011   01000001   01010100

a) Convert each binary number above to a hexadecimal number to encrypt the password 'CAT'.

....
[3]

b) The password 'DOG' is encrypted as 44 4F 47.
   i)   Convert the first encrypted letter to binary.

....
[1]

   ii) What password would be encrypted as 43 4F 44 45?

Hint: Look back at previous question parts.

....
[2]
[Total 6 marks]

3 Show that the hexadecimal equation $10 + 25 + 3A = 6F$ is correct.

Start by converting each number on the left hand side to denary.

....

....

....

....

[Total 4 marks]

4 Daniel is a programmer. He makes the following two claims about hex numbers.

Claim 1: "Hex is much easier to work with than binary."

Claim 2: "Converting from denary to hex is easier than converting from binary to hex."

Would other programmers agree with Daniel's claims? Explain your answers.

Claim 1: ....

....

....

Claim 2: ....

....

....

[Total 4 marks]

5 The function denary() converts one hexadecimal character to denary. (e.g. denary(F) = 15).

a) Calculate the value of denary(A) + denary(C).

....

[2]

b) Write an algorithm using denary() to convert any 2-digit hexadecimal into denary.

Think about splitting the 2-digit hexadecimal into separate characters.

[4]

[Total 6 marks]

Characters

1 Helena is writing a news article using a word processor.

a) Define the term 'character set'.

....

....

[1]

b) Complete the flow diagram to explain how Helena's computer recognises characters she enters.

```
( Start )
   |
   v
/ Key pressed / ---> [            ] ---> [            ] ---> / Character \ ---> ( Stop )
                                                             \ displayed /
```

[2]

[Total 3 marks]

2 The table on the right shows information on three standard character sets.

Character Set	Bit Length
ASCII	8
Extended ASCII	8
Unicode UTF-32	32

a) i) Describe in general how the bit length affects the size of the character set.

....

....

[1]

ii) Explain why ASCII and extended ASCII have the same bit length but have different numbers of characters in their character set.

....

....

[2]

iii) Ed claims that Unicode UTF-32 can represent 4 times as many characters as extended ASCII. Is he correct? Explain your answer.

....

....

[2]

b) Give **two** benefits of using Unicode UTF-32 to encode each character.

Benefit 1: ....

Benefit 2: ....

[2]

[Total 7 marks]

Section Seven — Data Representation

Storing Images

1   A computer screen displays images using pixels.

    a) Describe how the number of bits used per pixel affects the colours in an image.

      ....

      ....

      [2]

    b) How many bits per pixel would be needed for a pattern that uses 256 unique colours?

      ....

      [1]

    c) Explain which of the following images would need
       the greatest number of bits to represent all of the pixels.

       1 bit is needed to represent either O (white) or 1 (black).

       Image 1 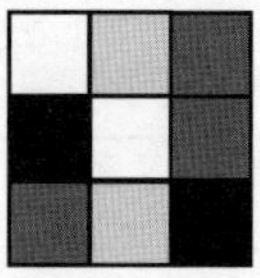   Image 2    Image 3

      ....

      ....

      ....

      [4]

      [Total 7 marks]

2   Duncan prints a 10 × 10 inch photograph with a resolution of 60 DPI.

    a) i)   Define the term 'resolution'.

       ....

       [1]

      ii)   Calculate the total number of pixels in Duncan's photograph.

       ....

       [2]

    b) Explain how decreasing the DPI would affect the image quality.

      ....

      ....

      [2]

    c) Explain the purpose of metadata in an image file.

      ....

      ....

      [2]

      [Total 7 marks]

Storing Sound

1 An analogue sound wave is being sampled to be stored in a digital format.

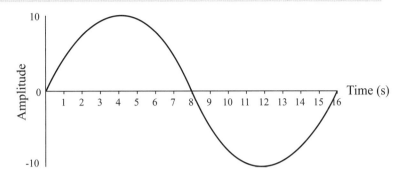

a) Add crosses to the sound wave above to show where samples would be taken if the sampling interval was 2 seconds.

[1]

b) Complete the flow diagram below to show the process of sampling.

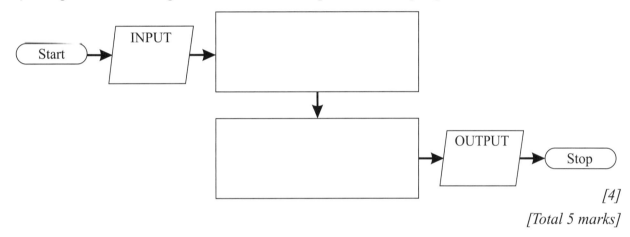

[4]

[Total 5 marks]

2 Jade records herself reading two extracts from a novel to use in an audiobook. The bit rates and sampling frequencies of each recording are shown below.

	Length	Bit Rate	Sampling Frequency
Extract 1	2 minutes	128 kbit/s	32 kHz
Extract 2	2 minutes	320 kbit/s	44.1 kHz

a) Explain which extract would have the better sound quality.

....

....

....

[2]

b) Give **one** drawback of using extract 2 rather than extract 1 for the audiobook.

....

[1]

[Total 3 marks]

Section Seven — Data Representation

Compression

	Lossless	Lossy
MP3		✔
FLAC	✔	

1   Ashmita wants to listen to a podcast. The podcast is available in two file formats — MP3 and FLAC.

a) Explain why compression is used for audio files.

....

....

[2]

b) Give **one** benefit and **one** drawback of downloading the FLAC file.

Benefit: ....

Drawback: ....

[2]

c) Ashmita downloads the podcast to her smartphone in the MP3 format. Give **two** reasons why she might have done this.

1 ....

....

2 ....

....

[4]

[Total 8 marks]

2   State and explain which type of compression would be most appropriate in these examples.

a) Uploading 100 holiday photographs to a social media account.

Type Of Compression: ....

Explanation: ....

....

[2]

b) Uploading a photograph of a model for a fashion magazine.

Type Of Compression: ....

Explanation: ....

....

[2]

[Total 4 marks]

Exam Practice Tip

It's good practice to relate your answers to the question that's being asked — if you're given an example of a person using lossy compression for an audio or image file, then it's best to answer how it will benefit **them**.
Think up some everyday examples where compression is used and how it is a benefit to the user in each case.

Section Seven — Data Representation

Mixed Questions

1   A program takes a binary number as an input and outputs a
hexadecimal number using the algorithm below.

- Input an 8-bit binary number.
- Complete a 2 place left shift on the binary number.
- Convert the new binary number to a hexadecimal number and output it.

a) What is the output if 10010110 is the input?

....

[3]

b) Find an 8-bit binary number that could be an input if the output is 2C?

.

....

[3]

[Total 6 marks]

2   A three hour radio broadcast transmits an analogue signal. A digital recording
of the broadcast is made by sampling different points of the analogue wave.

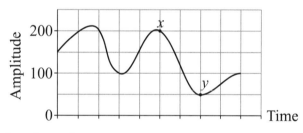

a) Complete the table below for point x.

	x	y
Denary Value		50
Binary Value		00110010
Hex Value		32

[3]

b) Explain how decreasing the sampling interval can affect the quality of the sound file.

....

....

[2]

c) Explain why lossy compression might be used on the sound file.

....

....

[2]

[Total 7 marks]

3 In extended ASCII, the binary code 01001010 represents the letter J and the binary code 01001011 represents the letter K.

> *The next character in the alphabet is one binary value greater than the previous character.*

a) i) What is the binary representation of the letter M?

....

[1]

ii) What is the hexadecimal representation of the letter P?

....

[2]

b) Unicode also uses binary code to represent different letters. Give **one** difference between the binary representations of a character in Unicode and in extended ASCII.

....

....

[1]

[Total 4 marks]

4 Florence is a graphic designer for a publishing company. The image editing software that she uses represents each unique colour as a six digit hex code.

> *A single hex character can represent 16 different values.*

a) As a power of 16, how many possible unique colours could Florence use?

....

[1]

b) Explain **one** benefit to programmers of using hex codes to represent the different colours.

....

....

[2]

Florence saves the same image as three different file types (shown in the table below). One of the file types uses lossy compression.

File Type	JPEG	PNG	TIF
Size	0.2 MB	1 MB	0.9 MB

c) State and explain which file type is most likely to be an example of lossy compression.

....

....

[2]

d) Evaluate the impact if Florence always used lossless compression to store all her images.

....

....

....

....

....

[6]

[Total 11 marks]

Section One —
Components of a Computer System

Page 4: Computer Systems

Warm-up

RAM, hard disk drive, graphics card, optical drive, cooling fan, motherboard, heat sink.

1 a) The physical components that make up a computer system. *[1 mark]*
      E.g. RAM stick / cooling fan / mouse *[1 mark]*
      Award a mark for any correct example of hardware.

   b) The programs or applications that a computer can run. *[1 mark]*
      E.g. word processor / Internet browser / file manager *[1 mark]*
      Award a mark for any correct example of software.

2 a) A computer system built into another device. *[1 mark]*

   b) Any **two** devices, e.g.
      • Dishwasher *[1 mark]*
      • Mp3 player *[1 mark]*
      • Digital thermometer *[1 mark]*
      • Washing machine *[1 mark]*
      • Manufacturing machinery *[1 mark]*
      [2 marks available in total]

   c) Any **two** benefits explained, e.g.
      • Embedded systems are far smaller than general purpose computers *[1 mark]* which means microwaves can be made more compact. *[1 mark]*
      • Embedded systems are cheaper to produce than general purpose computers *[1 mark]* which can reduce the costs / sale price of microwaves. *[1 mark]*
      • Embedded systems tend to be more reliable than general purpose computers *[1 mark]* which means that microwaves are less likely to break. *[1 mark]*
      [4 marks available in total]

Pages 5-6: The CPU

Warm-up

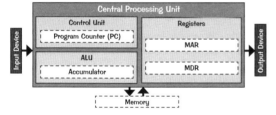

1 a) False *[1 mark]*
   b) True *[1 mark]*
   c) False *[1 mark]*
   d) True *[1 mark]*

2 a) Any **two** functions, e.g.
      • The control unit executes instructions. *[1 mark]*
      • It follows the fetch-decode-execute cycle. *[1 mark]*
      • It controls the flow of data within the CPU. *[1 mark]*
      • It controls the flow of data between the CPU and other parts of the computer system (such as memory, and input and output devices). *[1 mark]*
      [2 marks available in total]

   b) E.g. The ALU carries out arithmetic operations, e.g. addition, subtraction and multiplication (using repeated addition). *[1 mark]* It performs logic operations on binary data, such as AND, NOT, and OR. *[1 mark]*

   c) E.g. The cache is extremely fast memory in the CPU. *[1 mark]* It stores regularly used data or instructions. *[1 mark]* The CPU can access data stored in the cache much faster than retrieving it from RAM. *[1 mark]*

3 a) The registers are super fast memory that store tiny amounts of data or instructions *[1 mark]* that the CPU can access extremely quickly. *[1 mark]*

   b) The accumulator stores the results of calculations done by the ALU. *[1 mark]*
      The MAR holds any memory address about to be used by the CPU. *[1 mark]*
      The MDR holds data or instructions that have been fetched from / to be written to memory. *[1 mark]*

   c) If the program counter does not increment with each cycle, the memory address of the next instruction will always be the same, *[1 mark]* so the CPU would carry out the same instruction repeatedly. *[1 mark]*

4 E.g.
   Fetch:
   • The memory address from the program counter is copied to the MAR. *[1 mark]*
   • An instruction is fetched from memory / the address in the memory address register (MAR). *[1 mark]*
   • The fetched instruction is copied to the MDR. *[1 mark]*
   • The value in the program counter is changed to point to the address of the next instruction. *[1 mark]*
   Decode:
   • The fetched instruction is decoded by the control unit. *[1 mark]*
   • A new value may be loaded into the MAR / MDR to prepare for the execute step. *[1 mark]*
   Execute:
   • The decoded instruction is carried out / executed, *[1 mark]* e.g. data is loaded from memory / data is written to memory / a calculation is done / a program is halted. *[1 mark]*
   • The cycle is repeated. *[1 mark]*
   [6 marks available in total — fetch, decode and execute stages must all be covered for full marks.]

Page 7: Memory

1 Volatile memory is temporary memory — it requires power to retain its data content. *[1 mark]* Non-volatile memory retains its data content even when there is no power. *[1 mark]*

2 a) RAM holds any data that is currently in use, e.g. programs / OS / files / documents. *[1 mark]* It allows the CPU to directly access data much faster than if the data was on secondary storage. *[1 mark]*

   b) Any **two** reasons from:
      • The current amount of RAM may not meet the requirements for the software he wants to run. *[1 mark]*
      • His computer may be running slowly. *[1 mark]*
      • He may want to run more programs at once. *[1 mark]*
      • It may be constantly using virtual memory. *[1 mark]*
      [2 marks available in total]

3 a) E.g.
      • It loads the operating system. *[1 mark]*
      • It performs a variety of self-diagnostic tests on the hardware, e.g. testing RAM. *[1 mark]*
      • It checks for hardware connected to the computer. *[1 mark]*
      • It provides a basic user interface where some settings can be accessed, e.g. changing which storage device to load the OS from. *[1 mark]*
      [2 marks available in total]

   b) E.g. The BIOS must be stored in non-volatile memory, so its contents aren't lost when the computer is turned off. ROM is non-volatile memory, RAM is volatile. *[1 mark]* The contents of the BIOS should not be changed. ROM is read-only memory, but RAM is not and its contents can be altered. *[1 mark]*
      Be careful not to get non-volatile memory and ROM mixed up. ROM is just one type of non-volatile memory — there are other types of non-volatile memory that can be written to, e.g. flash memory.

c) Virtual memory is an area of secondary storage that the computer uses to store the contents of RAM temporarily *[1 mark]* when there isn't enough space in RAM to store necessary software / data. *[1 mark]* The computer will copy the items not currently in use from RAM to virtual memory, freeing up space in RAM. *[1 mark]*
[2 marks available in total]

d) E.g. Virtual memory can make a computer slow to respond, e.g. when switching between applications *[1 mark]*, because data transfer speeds from secondary storage are much slower than from RAM. *[1 mark]*

Page 8: CPU and System Performance

1 Any **three** components, e.g.
• Hard Disk Drive / secondary storage *[1 mark]*
• RAM *[1 mark]*
• CPU *[1 mark]*
• GPU *[1 mark]*
[3 marks available in total]

2 a) Clock speed is the number of instructions a CPU / processor core can carry out per second. *[1 mark]*

b) Cache is much faster than RAM. *[1 mark]* The larger the cache, the more data can be stored for quick access by the CPU, meaning the CPU should perform better. *[1 mark]*

c) E.g. Jackson's CPU has more cores than Will's CPU, which should mean better performance. *[1 mark]* It also has a larger cache than Will's, which should again lead to better CPU performance. *[1 mark]* On the other hand Will's CPU has a higher clock speed than Jackson's, so there is a chance that Will's may give better performance than Jackson's. *[1 mark]* Overall, it is hard to tell whether Will's CPU will offer better performance, therefore it seems unwise to buy Will's CPU, as it may be no better than Jackson's current one. *[1 mark]*
If you'd decided that Will's CPU was the best option, you'd still get the marks as long as you'd put together a sensible argument based on comparisons of the CPU specs.

d) E.g. Increasing the amount of RAM increases the amount of data / number of applications that the computer can hold in memory. *[1 mark]* Jackson may not use all of the current RAM in his computer, as he may use undemanding software or he may not open many programs at once *[1 mark]* so adding more RAM will not improve performance. *[1 mark]*
[2 marks available in total]

Pages 9-10: Secondary Storage

Warm-up

Uses a type of flash memory — Solid State Drive
Data is stored on a stack of magnetic disks — Hard Disk Drive
Data is stored as little pits on the surface — Optical Disc
Usually comes on a reel in a casette — Magnetic tape

1 a) Any **three** characteristics from:
• Capacity *[1 mark]*
• Reliability *[1 mark]*
• Cost *[1 mark]*
• Portability *[1 mark]*
• Data transfer speed *[1 mark]*
• Durability *[1 mark]*
[3 marks available in total]

b) i) Any **two** reasons, e.g.
• Flash storage / solid state storage is resistant to impacts, so is unlikely to be damaged when the action cam is in use. *[1 mark]*
• Flash storage can be very compact and lightweight. *[1 mark]*

ii) E.g.
• Magnetic hard disks are much larger and heavier than flash storage devices, making them unsuitable for a small, lightweight camera. *[1 mark]*
• Magnetic hard disks can be damaged greatly by impacts, so they would be unsuitable in an action camera. *[1 mark]*

2 E.g.
500 GB HDD:
• The HDD has a much greater capacity than the SSD. *[1 mark]*
• If she intends to store lots of data, e.g. photos / music / videos and 128 GB will not be enough storage space. *[1 mark]*
• The HDD is likely to cost far less per GB than the SSD. *[1 mark]*
• HDDs are said to have a longer read / write life than SSDs, so the HDD should be usable for longer. *[1 mark]*

128 GB SSD:
• The SSD will have a higher read / write speed than the HDD. *[1 mark]*
• If she needs a high performance drive for gaming the fast read / write speed may improve performance. *[1 mark]*
• If she wants the OS and programs to open and run as quickly as possible. *[1 mark]*
• The SSD will also be silent, whereas the HDD will make some noise. *[1 mark]*
[4 marks available — 2 marks for reasons to pick the HDD, 2 marks for reasons to pick the SSD]

3 a) $600 \times 7 \times 3 = 12\,600$ GB
$= 12.6$ TB *[1 mark]*

b) Magnetic tape *[1 mark]*

c) Any **two** advantages and **two** disadvantages, e.g.
Advantages:
• Magnetic tape is far cheaper per GB than other forms of secondary storage. *[1 mark]*
• Tape has a much larger data capacity than other forms of secondary storage, so is most suitable for storing many TB of data. *[1 mark]*
• Tape has a higher write speed than a HDD. *[1 mark]*
Disadvantages:
• It can take far longer to find a specific piece of data on tape, e.g. to recover certain files from a backup. *[1 mark]*
• Tape reading drives can be very expensive. *[1 mark]*
• Data can be corrupted if placed near a strong magnet. *[1 mark]*
[4 marks available in total]
Hard disk may be an acceptable answer in part b) if properly explained in part c). For example, the company would need several of them to store a month's worth of daily backups, and they are far more expensive than magnetic tapes, however they do offer some advantages over magnetic tape.

4 a) E.g.
• Secondary storage is needed to store data and software in the long term. *[1 mark]*
• Secondary storage is non-volatile memory, so retains data when there is no power. *[1 mark]*
• Computers could not function without permanent data storage, as all software and data would be lost when switched off. *[1 mark]*
• Secondary storage has a high capacity, so you can store a lot more data. *[1 mark]*
[3 marks available in total]

b) Any **two** advantages and **two** disadvantages, e.g.

Advantages:
- Optical discs have a low cost per GB. *[1 mark]*
- They are highly portable. *[1 mark]*
- They are durable against shock and water damage. *[1 mark]*

Disadvantages:
- They are very slow to write to. *[1 mark]*
- They require an optical drive to be read / written. *[1 mark]*
- They can be scratched easily. *[1 mark]*
- They have a low capacity compared to other forms of storage, e.g. flash memory cards. *[1 mark]*

[4 marks available in total]

Pages 11-13: Systems Software

Warm-up

```
E  M  J  R  C  O  D  E  R  D  A  I  K  Y  S  E
F [L] E  G  I [M] R  B  N  Z  B  O  V [I] A  U
W [I] F  M  E [A  N  D  R  O  I  D] A [O] L  M
A [N] T  B  Q [C] C  E  R  I  H  T  I [S] R  T
R [U] S  E  H [O] D [W  I  N  D  O  W  S] D  S
D [X] F  U  H [S] D  G  T  B  N  I  R  T  Z  B
```

1. a) Any **three** functions from:
   - The OS communicates with hardware via device drivers. *[1 mark]*
   - The OS provides a user interface. *[1 mark]*
   - The OS provides a platform for software / applications to run. *[1 mark]*
   - The OS allows a computer to multitask by controlling memory / CPU resources. *[1 mark]*
   - The OS deals with file and disk management. *[1 mark]*

   [3 marks available in total]

   b) Device drivers are pieces of software *[1 mark]* that allow the OS and hardware to communicate with each other. *[1 mark]*

   c) E.g.
   - They often allow different user accounts, giving each user access to their own personal data and desktop, which cannot be accessed by other users. *[1 mark]*
   - It may have anti-theft measures, like password or pin protection. *[1 mark]*
   - It may include encryption software, to allow users to protect their files. *[1 mark]*
   - It may include anti-virus software or a firewall to help protect against unauthorised users / software. *[1 mark]*

   [2 marks available in total]

2. E.g.
   - When applications / programs / files are opened, the OS moves the necessary parts to memory. *[1 mark]*
   - The OS will remove unneeded data from memory, e.g. when programs or files are closed. *[1 mark]*
   - The OS divides memory into segments. When different programs are used, their data is placed into different segments so that running applications can not write over or interfere with each other. *[1 mark]*
   - The OS organises the movement of data to-and-from virtual memory. *[1 mark]*
   - The OS divides CPU time between running applications / programs / processes, as it can only process one at a time. *[1 mark]*
   - The OS can prioritise CPU time for different programs in order for them to be processed in the most efficient order. *[1 mark]*

   [6 marks available in total — award a maximum of 4 marks for points about RAM or CPU time]

3. a) A graphical user interface allows the user to interact with the computer *[1 mark]* in a visual and intuitive way (e.g. through windows, menus and pointers). *[1 mark]*

   b) i) A command line interface allows the user to interact with a computer only by typing in commands from a set list. *[1 mark]*

   ii) Any **two** benefits from:
   - Command line interfaces give greater control / more options than GUIs. *[1 mark]*
   - They are less resource heavy than GUIs. *[1 mark]*
   - They can be used to automate processes using scripts. *[1 mark]*

   [2 marks available in total]

   c) E.g. To protect her sensitive data / files / contact info *[1 mark]* from malware / viruses / hackers / other users of her computer. *[1 mark]*

4. a) A full backup is where a copy is taken of every file on the system. *[1 mark]* An incremental backup is where only the files modified or created since the last backup are copied. *[1 mark]*

   b) E.g. The company could do full backups once a fortnight, *[1 mark]* but do incremental backups twice a day. *[1 mark]* Every 6 months, the company could use data compression software to compress the previous 6 month's backups in order to reduce the file size. *[1 mark]* Backup disks / tapes can then be placed in a fireproof box / locked safe or kept on a different site to protect against fire / flood / theft. *[1 mark]*

5. a) i) Utility software is software that helps to configure, optimise or maintain a computer. *[1 mark]*

   ii) Any **two** examples of utility software, e.g.
   - Disk defragmenter *[1 mark]*
   - System diagnostic tools *[1 mark]*
   - Anti-virus / anti-spyware *[1 mark]*
   - Backup software *[1 mark]*
   - Compression software *[1 mark]*
   - File management software *[1 mark]*

   [2 marks available in total]

   b) Any **two** types, e.g.
   - Temporary files *[1 mark]*
   - Cookies *[1 mark]*
   - Contents of the recycle bin *[1 mark]*
   - Offline webpages *[1 mark]*

   [2 marks available in total]

   c) i) E.g. Fragmentation occurs when files are moved, deleted or change in size. *[1 mark]* This leaves gaps on the hard disk. *[1 mark]* Files are split into chunks to fit them into the empty spaces. *[1 mark]*

   ii) E.g. When the hard disk is fragmented, it will take longer to read / write data on the hard disk. *[1 mark]* This in turn may slow down the computer. *[1 mark]*

   iii) E.g.
   - Defragmentation software reduces fragmentation by moving files on the hard disk. *[1 mark]*
   - The empty spaces / gaps are collected together. *[1 mark]*
   - Different bits of the same file are moved to be stored together. *[1 mark]*
   - This means the read / write heads won't need to move as far across the disk, so the read / write speed should improve. *[1 mark]*

   [3 marks available in total]

   iv) E.g. Disk clean-up will remove a number of files, so it will immediately leave gaps in the data stored on the hard disk, leading to fragmentation. *[1 mark]*

Answers

Page 14: Open Source and Proprietary Software

Warm-up

Mozilla® Firefox®, Android™, Linux and VLC are open source.
Microsoft® PowerPoint®, Adobe® Photoshop® and
Microsoft® Word are proprietary.

1 a) Proprietary software is software where only the compiled code
is released. *[1 mark]* Users are not allowed to modify, copy
or redistribute the software. *[1 mark]*

   b) Any **two** advantages of using proprietary software, e.g.
   - Comes with a warranty / customer support. *[1 mark]*
   - Should be well-tested and reliable. *[1 mark]*
   - Often very secure. *[1 mark]*

   Any **two** disadvantages of using proprietary software, e.g.
   - They may be paying for features they don't need. *[1 mark]*
   - The software may not exactly match their needs and it cannot
   be modified. *[1 mark]*
   - The software may not gain any new features through updates,
   as software companies will want to add it to their latest
   software as a selling point. *[1 mark]*

   [4 marks available in total]

2 a) E.g.
   - Open source software is software where the source code is
   made freely available. *[1 mark]*
   - Users can legally modify the source code to make their own
   version of the software. *[1 mark]*
   - Modified versions of the original source code can be shared
   under the same license as the original software. *[1 mark]*

   [2 marks available in total]

   b) Any **one** advantage and **one** disadvantage, e.g.

   Advantages:
   - It's usually free of charge. *[1 mark]* Free software can be
   used as a marketing tool — once the device is paid for, the
   user won't need to pay for any more software. *[1 mark]*
   - The software's source code can be adapted by users *[1 mark]*
   which may increase the functions of the TV-PC. *[1 mark]*
   - Popular open source software can be very reliable as
   problems may be quickly fixed by the community or
   developers *[1 mark]* meaning Ioteck may not need to work on
   / push out their own updates. *[1 mark]*

   Disadvantages:
   - They may have unpatched holes in security *[1 mark]*, which
   could worry customers and reduce sales of the product.
   [1 mark]
   - If there are problems with the open source software
   [1 mark] Ioteck may not have any support from the software
   developers. *[1 mark]*
   - Ioteck won't be able to make money by selling their own
   proprietary software, *[1 mark]* so they may make less
   profit from the product overall. *[1 mark]*

   [4 marks available in total]

Pages 15-16: Mixed Questions

1 a) Storage *[1 mark]*, GPU *[1 mark]*

   b) E.g. Hardeep should upgrade the RAM in his computer,
   [1 mark] as he only just has enough RAM to cover the
   minimum requirements, so the OS may not run very smoothly.
   [1 mark]

   c) RAM stores applications and data that is currently in use.
   [1 mark] As operating systems are running all the time, a
   large amount of the OS is kept in RAM. *[1 mark]*

   d) Any **two** features, e.g.
   - Large buttons and icons *[1 mark]* that can be pressed
   to open applications and windows. *[1 mark]*
   - Screens and menus *[1 mark]* that can be navigated /
   controlled by swiping or dragging with a finger. *[1 mark]*

   - Support for finger gestures *[1 mark]* such as pinching to
   zoom out / tap and hold to open additional options /
   four finger swipes to swap between apps etc. *[1 mark]*
   - Virtual on-screen keyboard *[1 mark]* to allow the user to type
   without attaching an external keyboard. *[1 mark]*

   [4 marks available in total]

   e) File types / extensions determine how the data is organised
   within the file. *[1 mark]* Compatible programs will know
   how to interpret data within certain file types. *[1 mark]*

2 a) i) E.g. Kirstie does not use any particularly resource-heavy
   software, so the XZ Monochrome would not be worth
   the cost. *[1 mark]* On the other hand, photo editing may
   benefit from using a quad-core processor instead of a dual
   core. *[1 mark]* As Kirstie likes to download HD TV shows,
   the 128 GB hard drive on the CGPC-Pro would probably be
   too small. *[1 mark]* Although Kirstie would benefit from
   a more powerful graphics card for photo editing, this gain
   would not be worth paying the extra £350 for. *[1 mark]*
   The CGPC3000 would be Kirstie's best option. *[1 mark]*

   [4 marks available in total]

   ii) E.g. Liam wants to be able to play the latest video games.
   These will be resource-heavy *[1 mark]* and require a
   powerful graphics card and CPU. *[1 mark]* Browsing the
   Internet and editing databases would be possible with all
   three computers, however the CGPCs would likely be too
   low powered for gaming. *[1 mark]* The computer with the
   most powerful CPU and dedicated graphics card is the XZ
   Monochrome, so that is Liam's best option. *[1 mark]* This
   may be the most expensive computer, but it is the only
   computer that fits his requirements. *[1 mark]*

   [4 marks available in total]

   *There are no strictly right or wrong answers here — just make
   sure that you clearly explain your reasoning.*

   b) Positive:
   E.g. Overclocking increases the clock speed of the processor,
   so it can carry out more instructions per second. *[1 mark]* This
   means the computer should run more quickly. *[1 mark]*

   Negative:
   E.g. Overclocking increases the heat output from a CPU
   [1 mark] which could lead to the CPU overheating, causing
   crashes, errors or even damage to the CPU. *[1 mark]*

Section Two — Networks

Page 17: Networks — LANs and WANs

1 a) A group of devices connected to share data, located on a single
site / over a small geographical area. *[1 mark]*

   b) Any **three** advantages, e.g.
   - The computers can share files more easily. *[1 mark]*
   - The computers can share the scanner / the computers can
   share hardware. *[1 mark]*
   - The business' six computers can share one Internet
   connection. *[1 mark]*
   - It is easier to install / update software. *[1 mark]*
   - The members of staff can communicate using instant
   messaging. *[1 mark]*
   - The business can store user accounts centrally. *[1 mark]*

   [3 marks available in total]

2 a) A WAN connects computers / LANs which are in different
geographical locations. *[1 mark]* The communication medium
is not owned by the company / the company hires the network
infrastructure. *[1 mark]*

   b) Any **two** benefits with matching explanations, e.g.
   - A WAN allows the schools to share data securely *[1 mark]*
   meaning they can share private and sensitive data like pupil
   records and test scores. *[1 mark]*

- A WAN has a dedicated amount of bandwidth *[1 mark]* meaning the schools can send large messages and files between them very quickly. *[1 mark]*
- A WAN allows storage to be centralised at one school *[1 mark]* providing an efficient way to store and access data which is valuable to all schools without the need to duplicate files. *[1 mark]*
[4 marks available in total]

c) Any **three** factors with matching explanations, e.g.
- Too many users on the network at the same time / heavy use without a sufficient amount of available bandwidth *[1 mark]* can cause congestion and slow the network. *[1 mark]*
- Wired connections tend to improve the network performance compared to wireless connections *[1 mark]* because they are generally faster and more reliable. *[1 mark]*
- Fibre optic cables have a greater performance capability than copper cables *[1 mark]* as the signal can travel over longer distances / the signal does not degrade / has higher bandwidth. *[1 mark]*
- Interference from other electronic or wireless devices can affect the performance of the network *[1 mark]* by decreasing the data speed / causing the network to slow down. *[1 mark]*
[6 marks available in total]

Page 18: Networks — Hardware
Warm-up

Wi-Fi® channel — A range of Wi-Fi® frequencies.
Coaxial cable — A type of copper cable that consists of a central wire protected by a metal shield.
CAT5e cable — Contains twisted pairs of copper wires.
Fibre optic cable — A type of cable that uses light to carry signals.

1) a) Network Interface Controller / Network Interface Card *[1 mark]*
   b) i) Ethernet is wired, Wi-Fi® is wireless *[1 mark]*
      ii) USB dongle / HDMI dongle / Wi-Fi® dongle *[1 mark]*
   c) i) A switch connects devices in a local area network *[1 mark]* by transmitting frames of data between them. *[1 mark]* Data is received by the switch and sent to the device with the correct MAC address. *[1 mark]*
      [2 marks available in total]
      ii) A router transmits data between networks *[1 mark]* in units called packets. *[1 mark]* A router can be used to connect a local area network (LAN) to the Internet. *[1 mark]*
      [2 marks available in total]
      iii) A Wireless Access Point (WAP) connects devices in a local area network *[1 mark]* wirelessly / using radio waves / using Wi-Fi®. *[1 mark]*

Page 19: Client-Server and Peer-to-Peer Networks
Warm-up

1 – The user clicks on a web page link in their web browser.
2 – The web browser asks the web server to send the web page data.
3 – The web server processes the request.
4 – The web server sends the web page data to the web browser.
5 – The web browser displays the web page for the user to view.

1) a) i) A Peer-to-Peer network is a group of devices connected to share data with each other *[1 mark]* in which all devices are equal / connected without a server. *[1 mark]*
      ii) Any **two** benefits, e.g.
      - The network is easy to maintain / no specialist knowledge is required to manage the network. *[1 mark]*
      - No extra expensive hardware is required to set up the network. *[1 mark]*
      - There is no dependence on a server / the network is not dependent on any one machine. *[1 mark]*
      Any **two** drawbacks, e.g.
      - Software needs to be installed / updated on individual machines rather than centrally. *[1 mark]*
      - Copying files from one peer computer to another creates duplicate files. *[1 mark]*
      - Peer computers may slow down when other devices are accessing them. *[1 mark]*
      - Peer computers are more likely to be turned off than a server, so files cannot be accessed at all times. *[1 mark]*
      [4 marks available in total]

   b) i) A Client-Server network is a group of devices connected to a central computer (server) *[1 mark]* which manages the network / processes requests from devices (clients) / stores files centrally. *[1 mark]*
      ii) Any **two** benefits, e.g.
      - User files are stored centrally so resources are used more efficiently / files are less likely to be duplicated. *[1 mark]*
      - Software is easier to install / update because it is centrally stored. *[1 mark]*
      - Servers are more reliable than peer machines. *[1 mark]*
      - It is easier to backup data centrally. *[1 mark]*
      - There is greater security as anti-malware software can be installed centrally / user access to files can be controlled. *[1 mark]*
      Any **two** drawbacks, e.g.
      - Client-Server networks are expensive to set up. *[1 mark]*
      - The business would need to employ an IT specialist to maintain the server / network. *[1 mark]*
      - If the server fails then all the client computers lose access to their files / client computers are dependent on the server. *[1 mark]*
      [4 marks available in total]

Pages 20-21: Network Topologies

1 a) E.g.
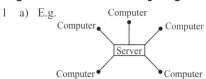
[2 marks for a correct fully labelled diagram, otherwise 1 mark for a correct but unlabelled diagram.]

   b) Any **three** advantages, e.g.
   - If a device or connection fails the rest of the network is unaffected. *[1 mark]*
   - Direct connections to switch / server mean all devices can transmit data at once. *[1 mark]*
   - Direct connections to switch / server mean there are no data collisions. *[1 mark]*
   - It's easy to add more devices to the network compared to other topologies. *[1 mark]*
   [3 marks available in total]

2 a) E.g.

Number of nodes	Star	Partial Mesh	Full Mesh
4	Switch		
5	Switch		
6	Switch		

[4 marks available — 1 mark for each correct diagram]
For the partial mesh topology, you'll get the mark as long as all nodes are indirectly linked to each other and there is more than one way to get between some of the nodes.

b) Any **one** advantage,
E.g. If a single device or connection fails on a mesh network, the network still functions as data can go along a different route. *[1 mark]* In a star network, central switch failure will cause the whole network to fail / a single connection failure will cut that device off from the network. *[1 mark]*

Any **one** disadvantage,
E.g. Devices in a mesh network need many more connections than in a star network. *[1 mark]* This requires a lot of cabling which can be expensive / impractical for networks with a large number of nodes. *[1 mark]*

3 a) If the central switch fails, users will be unable to access files on other servers *[1 mark]* because there will be no connections between any of the servers. *[1 mark]*

b) E.g.
• Connecting servers in a mesh network means that if one connection fails, there are other routes to connect the servers. *[1 mark]* This means the network can still operate fully and all the computers can access data on all servers. *[1 mark]*
• Adding an extra server to a mesh network would be more complicated *[1 mark]* because it would need to be connected to all of the other servers rather than just the switch. *[1 mark]*
• Some connections would be redundant most of the time *[1 mark]* as the servers would communicate using the quickest or most direct route. *[1 mark]*
[4 marks available in total]

Pages 22-23: Network Protocols

1 a) A set of rules for how devices communicate. *[1 mark]*

b) • The sending device splits the data up into smaller units called <u>packets</u>. *[1 mark]*
• Each packet is given a <u>packet number</u> *[1 mark]* to show the order of the data.
• The direction each packet takes to reach its destination is decided by pieces of hardware called <u>routers</u> *[1 mark]* using the <u>IP / Internet</u> protocol. *[1 mark]*
• Packets sometimes arrive at the receiving device in the wrong order. The receiving device uses the <u>packet number</u> *[1 mark]* to put them in the right order.

2 a) E.g.
• IP addresses are used to identify devices on a network / on the Internet. *[1 mark]*
• Routers use IP addresses to direct data packets to the correct destination. *[1 mark]*
[2 marks available in total]

b) i) E.g.
• Jonathan's laptop checks periodically that all packets have been received. *[1 mark]*
• If Jonathan's laptop does not receive all the packets in a certain amount of time it sends a timeout message back to the smartphone. *[1 mark]*
• Mahindar's smartphone resends the email / packet. *[1 mark]*
• Jonathan's laptop uses the packet numbers to reassemble them into the correct order. *[1 mark]*
[3 marks available in total]

ii) E.g.
• Mahindar's smartphone includes a checksum number in each of the data packets. *[1 mark]*
• Jonathan's laptop recalculates the checksum number of each packet when they arrive. *[1 mark]*
• The checksum numbers will not match for the corrupted packet. *[1 mark]*
• Jonathan's laptop sends a message to Mahindar's smartphone to resend the data. *[1 mark]*
• Mahindar's smartphone resends the email / packet. *[1 mark]*
[3 marks available in total]

3

Protocol	Function
TCP	Sets rules for how devices connect on the network / splits data into packets / reassembles packets into original data / checks data is sent and delivered.
IP	Responsible for packet switching.
HTTP	Used by web browsers to access websites / communicate with web servers.
HTTPS	A more secure version of HTTP.
FTP	Used to access, edit and move files on other devices.
SMTP	Used to send emails / transfer emails between servers.
IMAP	Used to retrieve emails from a server. The user downloads a copy of the email and the server holds the original email until the user deletes it.
POP3	Used to retrieve emails from a server. The server holds the email until the user downloads it, at which point the server deletes it.

[8 marks available in total — 1 mark for each correct answer]

4 a) E.g.
• A MAC address is a unique identifier. *[1 mark]*
• A MAC address is assigned to the hardware of every network-enabled device. *[1 mark]*
• MAC addresses are used to direct data to the right device on a network. *[1 mark]*
[2 marks available in total]

b) i) A layer of network protocols is a group of protocols with similar functions *[1 mark]* that cover one particular aspect of network communications. *[1 mark]*

ii) E.g.
• Data link layer *[1 mark]* Function: passing data over the physical network / sending data bits as electrical signals over cables, wireless and other hardware. *[1 mark]*
• Network layer *[1 mark]* Function: making connections between networks / directing data packets / handling traffic. *[1 mark]*
• Transport layer *[1 mark]* Function: controlling data flow / splitting data into packets / checking packets are correctly sent and delivered. *[1 mark]*
• Application layer *[1 mark]* Function: turning data into websites and other applications / turning websites and other applications into data. *[1 mark]*
[2 marks available in total]

iii) Any **three** benefits, e.g.
• Layers break network communication into manageable pieces. *[1 mark]*
• Layers allow developers to focus on one area of the network without worrying about the others. *[1 mark]*
• Layers are self-contained. *[1 mark]*
• There are set rules for each layer. *[1 mark]*
• Layers allow interoperability / layers make companies produce compatible, universal hardware and software. *[1 mark]*
[3 marks available in total]

Page 24: Networks — The Internet

Warm up

Protocol — https
Domain name — www.cgpbooks.co.uk
Path to the specific page — student / books_gcse

1 a) The Internet is a global network of networks. *[1 mark]* The World Wide Web is a collection of websites hosted on web servers. *[1 mark]*

b) A Domain Name Server translates a website's domain name into its IP address / stores domain names of websites in a directory. *[1 mark]*

2 a) E.g.
• A virtual network is a software-based network. *[1 mark]*
• A virtual network is created by partitioning off some of the physical network's bandwidth to create a separate network. *[1 mark]*

b) E.g.
- A VPN would allow the company to share data between the two sites. *[1 mark]*
- The company can send data over a VPN more securely than they could over the Internet. *[1 mark]*
- A VPN allows staff at one site to remotely log in to a computer based at the other site. *[1 mark]*
- A VPN is cheaper to maintain compared to a wide area network (WAN). *[1 mark]*
- A VPN would allow staff to log in and work from home or whilst travelling. *[1 mark]*

[2 marks available in total]

3 Points you might include:

Advantages of the cloud
- Users can access files from any location, so the company and authors can work on the same files without having to email or post manuscripts.
- Cloud storage is managed by the hosting company which will be a cheaper alternative to managing their own storage.
- The hosting company manages the security of data in the cloud, so the publishing company does not need to spend time securing its data.
- The hosting company is responsible for backing up data in the cloud, so the publishing company does not need to invest in any additional hardware to ensure data is backed up correctly.
- The publishing company could use cloud-based software rather than installing it on their machines and keeping it up to date. This could give writers access to the same software.

Disadvantages of the cloud
- An Internet connection is required to access the cloud, and maintaining a steady Internet connection can be difficult in rural areas.
- The publishing company is dependent on the hosting company for the security in the cloud, meaning the publishing company has very little control over the security of its data.
- The publishing company is dependent on the hosting company for backing up their data.
- Cloud software may require a monthly subscription which may be more expensive than buying computer licences.

How to mark your answer:
- Two or three brief points with very little explanation. *[1-2 marks]*
- Three or four detailed points covering both advantages and disadvantages. *[3-4 marks]*
- Five or more detailed points that form a well-written, balanced discussion, covering both advantages and disadvantages. *[5-6 marks]*

Make sure your answer is relevant to the situation you're given — the company in the question has particular needs and qualities which you shouldn't ignore.

Pages 25-27: Network Security Threats

Warm-up

Ransomware — Encrypts the data on the user's device, making them pay money to the hacker in exchange for the key to decrypt it.
Virus — Spread by users copying infected files.
Rootkit — Alters permissions and access levels on the user's device.
Spyware — Secretly monitors user actions.
Trojan — Malware disguised as legitimate software.
Scareware — Tells the user their computer is infected with malware in order to make them follow malicious links to "fix" the problem.
Worm — Self-replicating malware.

1 a) i) A passive attack is a network attack where the hacker monitors network traffic and intercepts sensitive information. *[1 mark]*
   ii) E.g. Using data encryption to prevent intercepted data from being read. *[1 mark]*

b) A denial-of-service attack floods the network server / website with useless data *[1 mark]* so the user or their site visitors cannot access part of their network or website. *[1 mark]*

c) The bank can use pentesting to identify potential weaknesses in the bank's security. *[1 mark]* They'll then use this information to patch or fix the weaknesses. *[1 mark]*

2 a) Phishing *[1 mark]*

b) Phishing emails are used to trick people into thinking they are emails from legitimate organisations *[1 mark]* so that they give the criminals their personal information, e.g. account login details. *[1 mark]*

c) The email attachment could be a virus or other type of malware. *[1 mark]* Opening the attachment would therefore activate the virus or malware / cause the virus or malware to infect the device. *[1 mark]*

3 a) A firewall can stop malware and hackers from accessing the school's network *[1 mark]* by blocking traffic that is identified as suspicious. *[1 mark]*

b) E.g.
- Different user access levels prevent students from accessing the same data as teachers, including sensitive data like their peers' personal information. *[1 mark]*
- Different user access levels prevent a student from maliciously deleting or editing data. *[1 mark]*
- Different user access levels prevent students accidentally deleting or editing important files. *[1 mark]*
- Different user access levels allow network administrators to flexibly change the amount of access students and staff have to certain files. *[1 mark]*

[3 marks available in total]

c) i) A brute force attack is a type of attack on a network which uses trial and error to crack passwords *[1 mark]* by employing automated software to produce hundreds of likely combinations. *[1 mark]*

   ii) Any **two** measures, e.g.
- The school can lock access to user accounts after a certain number of password attempts. *[1 mark]*
- The school can ensure that strong passwords are used / the school can ensure that passwords are long enough / the school can ensure that passwords are made of a mix of different types of character. *[1 mark]*
- The school can add additional security checks, like using a secret question or CAPTCHA test. *[1 mark]*

[2 marks available in total]

4 a) i) E.g.
- An SQL Query is entered into the input box of a website. *[1 mark]*
- The input box was not designed for that query but it is permitted by the website's / database's code. *[1 mark]*
- The inserted code runs a database query that can give unauthorised access to the whole or part of the database. *[1 mark]*

[2 marks available in total]

   ii) SQL injection can be prevented by using stronger input validation *[1 mark]* so that only the intended input type will be accepted. *[1 mark]*

b) E.g.
- A criminal calls one of the supermarket's employees and pretends to be a member of the supermarket's IT team. *[1 mark]*
- The criminal gains the employee's trust through the use of jargon, information related to the supermarket or flattery. *[1 mark]*
- The criminal persuades the employee to disclose their account details, giving the criminal access to their company account. *[1 mark]*

[2 marks available in total]

94

5 Points you might include:

<u>The threats posed to the firm's network</u>
- Hackers could use rootkits, spyware and other malware to steal confidential information.
- Employees unaware of the potential dangers could be tricked into giving criminals sensitive information through social engineering.
- Disgruntled employees could use their position to attack the network, e.g. by releasing malware onto the network from a USB drive.
- Hackers with packet sniffers or other similar tools could intercept and read information entering or leaving the company's network.
- Hackers could use a brute force attack to crack weak passwords.

<u>What a good network policy would include</u>
- Automatic encryption of all data leaving and entering the network.
- Installing anti-malware and firewall software.
- Regular penetration testing to find problems in the network security.
- Education of employees on the dangers of social engineering.
- Mandatory use of strong passwords / passwords that are changed regularly.
- An acceptable use policy that all employees must sign.
- Controlling physical access to hardware / the network, e.g. keeping servers in locked rooms.
- Different user access levels given to different groups of users.

<u>How a good network policy would prevent potential attacks on the firm's network.</u>
- A firewall would prevent harmful malware from entering the network.
- Education of employees could prevent social engineering.
- Different user access levels and physical security measures could limit the dangers of an insider attack.
- Encrypting data could prevent intercepted data from being read by hackers and criminals.
- Using strong passwords could prevent successful brute force attacks.

How to mark your answer:
- Two or three brief points with very little explanation. *[1-2 marks]*
- Three to five detailed points covering at least two of the three suggested topics. *[3-5 marks]*
- Six or more detailed points that form a well-written, balanced discussion, covering all of the suggested topics. *[6-8 marks]*

Pages 28-29: Mixed Questions

1 a) i) <u>Ethernet</u> is a network protocol used on wired networks. *[1 mark]*
<u>WPA2</u> is a security protocol used on wireless LANs. *[1 mark]*

ii) Any **one** difference, e.g.
- CAT5e twisted pair cables use four twisted copper wires *[1 mark]* whereas coaxial cable uses one single copper wire. *[1 mark]*
- CAT5e cables prevent interference by twisting the wires together *[1 mark]* whereas coaxial cable uses a braided metallic shield to prevent interference. *[1 mark]*

[2 marks available in total]

iii) E.g.
The Leeds studio's wired setup:
- Wired connections have a more reliable performance as there is no loss of signal no matter where the devices are in the building. *[1 mark]*
- Wired connections are more restrictive as it is harder to add new devices / access the network while moving through the building. *[1 mark]*

The York studio's wireless setup:
- Wireless connections are easier for the employees to connect to (e.g. no need for cables to add a laptop or mobile device to the network). *[1 mark]*
- Wireless connections can suffer from signal problems caused by building interference or interference from other wireless signals nearby. *[1 mark]*

To get all four marks, you'll need one advantage and one disadvantage for wired connections, as well as one advantage and one disadvantage for wireless connections.

b) i) Any **one** advantage, e.g.
- Fibre optic cables tend to have greater bandwidth / can carry more data than copper cables. *[1 mark]*
- Fibre optic cables can carry data over longer distances / don't suffer signal degradation or interference. *[1 mark]*
- Fibre optic cables are easier to maintain than copper cables so cost less in the long term. *[1 mark]*

[1 mark available in total]

ii) E.g.
- Laying its own cables between Leeds and York could be too expensive for the company. *[1 mark]*
- Leased lines are likely to be more reliable and faster than other WAN connections. *[1 mark]*

[1 mark available in total]

2 a) The use of online servers provided by a hosting company to store files and software. *[1 mark]*

b) E.g.
- Laptop / web browser sends a request to the cloud server, to send the image. *[1 mark]*
- The cloud server processes the request. *[1 mark]*
- The cloud server replies with the image. *[1 mark]*

[2 marks available in total]

c) i) E.g.
- The cloud server splits the image into packets. *[1 mark]*
- Each packet is given control information, including the IP addresses of the server and the laptop. *[1 mark]*
- The server calculates a checksum number for each packet. *[1 mark]*
- Each packet is given a packet number to show the order of the data. *[1 mark]*
- Each router reads the control information of the packet and decides which way to send the data. *[1 mark]*
- IP protocol governs packet switching. *[1 mark]*
- The way the data is sent changes according to network traffic so packets take different routes to their destination. *[1 mark]*
- Packets arrive at their destination in the wrong order. *[1 mark]*
- The receiving device puts the packets in the right order using the packet numbers on each packet. *[1 mark]*
- The receiving device recalculates the checksum. *[1 mark]*
- If all packets are successfully delivered and the checksums match, a receipt confirmation is sent back to the sending device. *[1 mark]*

[6 marks available in total]

Answers

ii) E.g.
- There are many possible routes the data can take *[1 mark]* so the data can reach the destination even if there is heavy network traffic. *[1 mark]*
- Splitting data into small packets allows different parts of the data to be routed separately *[1 mark]* which is more flexible than sending the whole file in one go. *[1 mark]*
[2 marks available in total]

d) i) A set of rules and procedures the organisation will follow to ensure their network is protected against attacks and unauthorised access. *[1 mark]*

ii) E.g.
- Network forensics are investigations undertaken to find the cause of attacks on a network. *[1 mark]*
- To conduct network forensics, an organisation needs to have a system of capturing data packets as they enter their network. *[1 mark]*
- After the network is attacked, data packets can be analysed to discover how the network was attacked. *[1 mark]*
- The information gained from network forensics can be used to decide how to prevent future attacks. *[1 mark]*
[3 marks available in total]

Section Three — Issues

Pages 30-32: Ethical and Cultural Issues
Warm-up

	Censorship	Surveillance
A business monitors what their employees view online.		✓
A country's government blocks access to Facebook®.	✓	
A government agency intercepts emails containing certain words.		✓
A school restricts access to harmful websites.	✓	
An Internet Service Provider collects data on browsing habits.		✓

1 a) An individual or group of people with an interest in a particular decision / are affected by a particular outcome. *[1 mark]*

b) Any **two** stakeholders, e.g.
- Business owners / managers *[1 mark]* — positive *[1 mark]* because they receive increased profits and do not have to pay the staff. *[1 mark]*
- Checkout staff *[1 mark]* — negative *[1 mark]* because they have lost their jobs. *[1 mark]*

2 Any **two** health risks, e.g.
- Eyestrain *[1 mark]* can be prevented by using suitable lighting / keeping the screen a good distance away from your eyes / taking regular breaks. *[1 mark]*
- Repetitive Strain Injury / RSI *[1 mark]* can be prevented by having a correct posture / arranging your desk appropriately / taking regular breaks. *[1 mark]*
- Back problems *[1 mark]* can be prevented by having a correct posture / using an adjustable chair / using a foot rest / using an adjustable monitor. *[1 mark]*
[4 marks available in total]

3 a) Cyberbullying: The use of social media to deliberately harm someone else. *[1 mark]*
Trolling: Causing arguments or provoking anger and frustration online. *[1 mark]*

b) Any **two** reasons, e.g.
- The Internet and social media can give people greater anonymity than they would have in real life. *[1 mark]*
- The ease of communicating online means people say things without thinking. *[1 mark]*
- There are often a lack of consequences or punishment for somebody who behaves badly online. *[1 mark]*
[2 marks available in total]

c) Any **one** example, e.g.
- Social media encourages users to share personal information and photographs with others, who may only be distant friends or colleagues *[1 mark]* so has made it more socially acceptable to share personal information. *[1 mark]*
- Social media websites have lax privacy settings by default *[1 mark]* making it difficult for users to protect their privacy. *[1 mark]*
- Users have no choice but to agree to the social media company's privacy agreement before using the website *[1 mark]* making it harder for users to control their privacy if they want to join in. *[1 mark]*
[2 marks available in total]

d) Any **one** positive impact, e.g.
- Social media allows friends to keep in touch *[1 mark]* so helps maintain or improve our social lives. *[1 mark]*
- Social media allows people to communicate with each other cheaply *[1 mark]* so there is no need to pay high phone bills. *[1 mark]*
- Social media allows you to share images and other media online quickly and easily *[1 mark]* so you do not need to invest in physical copies of media to share them with others. *[1 mark]*
- Social media allows anybody with access to the Internet the ability to express their views and opinions *[1 mark]* giving a voice to those who are often ignored. *[1 mark]*
[2 marks available in total]

4 a) E.g.
- Censoring certain websites can prevent employees from viewing harmful material, e.g. gambling, hate speech or pornography. *[1 mark]* Such material can cause harm, offense or distress to their colleagues so censoring the material helps to prevent this. *[1 mark]*
- Censoring certain websites can ensure employees are focused on their work *[1 mark]* improving the productivity for the business they are working for. *[1 mark]*
- Censoring certain websites can prevent employees from accessing illegal sites. *[1 mark]* This means the company cannot be considered legally culpable in allowing their employees to view such material. *[1 mark]*
- Censoring certain websites can infringe upon the freedom of employees *[1 mark]* as it restricts which websites they can access. *[1 mark]*
- Censorship shows the business has a lack of trust in their employees *[1 mark]* which may cause demotivation and resentment. *[1 mark]*
[4 marks available in total]

b) E.g.
- Monitoring and surveillance could restrict the freedom of employees *[1 mark]* as they may feel they cannot access certain websites. *[1 mark]*
- Monitoring and surveillance of emails and messages sent from a work computer can infringe upon employees' privacy *[1 mark]* because it means they cannot communicate with anyone confidentially / they may be using email or messaging services to send personal information to family members, doctors, etc. *[1 mark]*
- Employees may not be told about whether they are being monitored or how much of their activity is being monitored *[1 mark]* which raises issues of transparency and trust between the company and the employee. *[1 mark]*

[4 marks available in total]

It's important to know the different effects that censorship and surveillance can have — censorship restricts people's freedom, while surveillance damages their privacy.

5 a) E.g.
- The Internet / social media / email mean Tom can be contacted at any time of day. *[1 mark]*
- Tom may be expected to carry a smartphone at all times so he can be contacted by his boss at all times. *[1 mark]*
- Tom's smartphone may alert him when he receives work emails from clients. These can be hard to ignore. *[1 mark]*

[2 marks available in total]

b) E.g.
- Companies try to influence people into using their new product, e.g. by using advertisements. *[1 mark]*
- Many children may feel peer pressure to buy the new devices for fear of being bullied by their classmates. *[1 mark]*
- Parents can feel pressured to buy the latest technology for their children. *[1 mark]*

[2 marks available in total]

c) Any **one** reason, e.g.
- They might not have a lot of money *[1 mark]* so cannot afford to buy expensive electronic devices. *[1 mark]*
- They might live in a rural area *[1 mark]* so could have poor network coverage. *[1 mark]*
- They might have little knowledge of how to use the Internet or electronic devices *[1 mark]* so feel too intimidated to use them. *[1 mark]*

[2 marks available in total]

6 Points you might include:

Stakeholders
- Manufacturing businesses can cut costs by getting the same products made without having to pay any wages.
- Workers in the manufacturing sector could become unemployed, as robots take over their jobs.
- Consumers could be able to buy the same products for less, as the costs involved in making them could be lower.

Technology
- The hardware and software of robots may not be sophisticated enough to fully replicate the work of human employees.
- The increased use of robots in the workplace could help improve them as problems can be identified and fixed.
- Successful use of robots in manufacturing could lead to their application in other areas of work.

Ethical issues
- Manufacturing businesses could leave hundreds of people without jobs in order to pursue profit.
- There is currently a lack of awareness and rules around the use of robots in the workplace.
- By allowing robots to do the routine jobs, workers are free to do more interesting, creative and fulfilling work.
- New jobs are created to program, maintain and manufacture the robots.
- Robots can perform hazardous tasks, meaning there could be fewer injuries in the workplace.

How to mark your answer:
- Two or three brief points with very little explanation. *[1-2 marks]*
- Three or four detailed points covering at least two of: stakeholders, technology and ethical issues. *[3-4 marks]*
- Five or more detailed points that form a well-written, balanced discussion, covering all of: stakeholders, technology and ethical issues. *[5-6 marks]*

Pages 33-34: Environmental Issues
Warm-up
- Plastic
- Silver
- Platinum
- Gold
- Copper
- Mercury

1 a) A material which is extracted from the earth / a material which is the basis for other products. *[1 mark]*

b) Any **two** effects, e.g.
- Extracting raw materials depletes scarce natural resources. *[1 mark]*
- The process of raw material extraction causes pollution. *[1 mark]*
- Some raw materials used in electronic devices are difficult to recycle so end up in landfill. *[1 mark]*
- Some raw materials used in electronic devices are toxic after they are disposed of. *[1 mark]*

[2 marks available in total]

2 a) E-waste is discarded computer material / discarded electronic material. *[1 mark]*

b) Any **two** reasons, e.g.
- Many devices are portable, so can be broken easily, for example by dropping them. *[1 mark]*
- Many devices are not built to last more than a few years. *[1 mark]*
- It is often cheaper to replace a device than it is to repair it. *[1 mark]*
- Device manufacturers release new devices on a regular basis and use advertisements to influence people into buying them. *[1 mark]*
- People often want to buy the newest technology and are happy to discard their old devices regularly. *[1 mark]*
- Retailers only provide short warranties on many devices. *[1 mark]*
- Many people feel pressured by their peers to upgrade to the latest device. *[1 mark]*

[2 marks available in total]

c) E.g.
- E-waste is sent to landfill sites *[1 mark]* where toxic chemicals can enter groundwater / harm wildlife. *[1 mark]*
- The short life span of devices also means more natural resources have to be extracted to make new devices *[1 mark]* which causes pollution and depletes scarce resources. *[1 mark]*
- Devices use up a lot of energy / electricity *[1 mark]* which is created using non-renewable resources. *[1 mark]*

[4 marks available in total]

d) E.g.
- People can take devices to local collection facilities to be correctly disposed of according to WEEE regulations *[1 mark]* rather than throwing them out with general waste. *[1 mark]*
- The government can put pressure on companies or local authorities to ensure WEEE regulations are being followed. *[1 mark]* The government can set recycling targets to increase the amount of e-waste that is recycled. *[1 mark]*
- Old devices can be refurbished and reused *[1 mark]* and their raw materials can be recycled. *[1 mark]*

[2 marks available in total]

Answers

3 a) Any **two** ways, e.g.
   - Users sometimes leave devices idle / on standby. *[1 mark]*
   - Many devices are inefficient (either by design or through lack of servicing) meaning they generate excessive heat, which requires energy to remove through air conditioning. *[1 mark]*
   - Users sometimes leave their devices on charge longer than they need to. *[1 mark]*
   - Many devices, like servers, very rarely run at their full capacity. This means they are using lots of energy but not doing much with it, so the energy is wasted. *[1 mark]*
   [2 marks available in total]

   b) E.g.
   - Manufacturers can include sleep or hibernation modes in new devices *[1 mark]* to reduce their energy consumption when they are idle. *[1 mark]*
   - Manufacturers can design devices to be more energy efficient, *[1 mark]* for example to minimise the amount of heat they generate. *[1 mark]*
   [2 marks available in total]

   c) E.g.
   - Most energy comes from non-renewable sources like coal, gas and oil. *[1 mark]* These resources are scarce. *[1 mark]* Extracting these resources / burning these resources in power stations causes pollution. *[1 mark]*
   - As developing countries become developed countries, their energy consumption will increase. *[1 mark]*
   - The use of energy from non-renewable resources will accelerate climate change. *[1 mark]*
   - The world will need to get more of its energy from renewable sources (like solar, wind and wave) if it is to fulfil the worldwide demand for energy in the future. *[1 mark]*
   - More nuclear power stations may need to be built, to which many people are opposed. *[1 mark]*
   [4 marks available in total]
   This last Q part isn't about how computers use electricity. It's about the bigger picture of how to meet the increasing worldwide demand for energy.

4 Points you might include:
   Energy
   - The new monitor would be more energy efficient, so there would be less waste of electricity.
   - A more energy efficient monitor would mean less electricity would need to be produced for it, which means less pollution.
   - The energy saved by using a more energy efficient model may not be enough to make up for the energy used in the creation of the new monitor, which defeats the point of buying an energy efficient monitor.

   E-waste
   - Throwing away the current monitor would create more e-waste, which could end up in a landfill site. Toxic chemicals in the monitor could leak, causing harm to wildlife and the environment.
   - Shaun could look to recycle parts of the monitor or give it to somebody else so they can reuse it.
   - It is not clear whether Shaun will keep the new monitor for any longer than his previous monitor. His new monitor could break or he could decide to replace it with yet another monitor.

   Natural resources
   - The new monitor will use raw materials, which adds to the depletion of natural resources.
   - The extraction of raw materials requires more energy, which causes more pollution.

   How to mark your answer:
   - Two or three brief points with very little explanation. *[1-2 marks]*
   - Three or four detailed points covering at least two of: energy, e-waste and natural resources. *[3-4 marks]*
   - Five or more detailed points that form a well-written, balanced discussion, covering all of: energy, e-waste and natural resources. *[5-6 marks]*

Pages 35-37: Computer Legislation
Warm-up
- A hospital holds the medical records of its patients so they can be treated — Data Protection Act 1998
- A criminal hacks into a broadband company's network and steals its customers' account details — Computer Misuse Act 1990
- A request is made to a university to release information regarding the amount their vice chancellor is paid — Freedom of Information Act 2000
- A polling company holds data on members of the public for a survey it is conducting — Data Protection Act 1998
- An employee accesses their manager's network account and deletes company data — Computer Misuse Act 1990

1 a) A data subject is someone whose personal data is stored on somebody else's computer system. *[1 mark]*

   b) Any **three** principles, e.g.
   - Data must only be used in a fair and lawful way. *[1 mark]*
   - Data must only be used for the specified purpose. *[1 mark]*
   - Data should be adequate, relevant and not excessive for the specified use. *[1 mark]*
   - Data must be accurate and kept up to date. *[1 mark]*
   - Data should not be kept longer than is necessary. *[1 mark]*
   - The rights of the data subject must be observed. *[1 mark]*
   - Data should be kept safe and secure. *[1 mark]*
   - Data should not be transferred abroad without adequate protection. *[1 mark]*
   [3 marks available in total]

2 a) A way of protecting intellectual property / a way of protecting something that has been created / a way of protecting written and recorded content, e.g. books, music, films, software and video games. *[1 mark]*

   b) Works in the public domain are those whose copyright has expired / works which do not have any copyright attached to them *[1 mark]* meaning they can be shared and copied without normal copyright rules being applied. *[1 mark]*

3 a) Hayley needs to contact the owner of the image *[1 mark]* and request permission to use it. *[1 mark]* Hayley will have to follow the copyright holder's request / acknowledge the source of the image / may have to pay a fee. *[1 mark]*

   b) E.g.
   - They might want the photograph to be shared so it is seen by as many people as possible. *[1 mark]* Those sharing the photograph might have to credit the photographer, allowing the photographer to raise their profile. *[1 mark]*
   - They might want the photograph to be modified *[1 mark]* so it can be used as part of another creative work, e.g. a magazine. *[1 mark]*
   [2 marks available in total]

   c) i)   The copyright holder must be given credit. *[1 mark]*
      ii) The work cannot be used for financial or commercial gain. *[1 mark]*
      iii) Modified works can only be distributed with the same terms as those applied to the original. *[1 mark]*
      iv) The work cannot be modified or built upon. *[1 mark]*

98

d) Any **two** ways, e.g.
  - The solicitor did not acknowledge Hayley *[1 mark]* which breaks the attribution condition of her Creative Commons licence. *[1 mark]*
  - By including it in an advertisement, the solicitor used the photograph for commercial gain *[1 mark]* which breaks the non-commercial condition of Hayley's Creative Commons licence. *[1 mark]*
  - The solicitor shared the photograph without attaching the same copyright terms to it as Hayley's original *[1 mark]* which breaks the share-alike condition of her Creative Commons licence. *[1 mark]*

  [4 marks available in total]
  Use your knowledge on the different Creative Commons licences and the information given in the question to show how the solicitor infringed Hayley's copyright.

4 a) The council should send the information to the member of public who requested it *[1 mark]* unless there is a reason to withhold it, e.g. the information concerns national security. *[1 mark]*

  b) E.g.
  - The hackers broke the Computer Misuse Act 1990 *[1 mark]* by gaining unauthorised access to the council's network *[1 mark]* in order to commit a crime / steal information. *[1 mark]*
  - The council may have broken the Data Protection Act 1998 *[1 mark]* because they were holding information about members of the public for longer than necessary. *[1 mark]* They may also have neglected to keep the data safe and secure *[1 mark]* and the release of the data may have caused data subjects distress. *[1 mark]*

  [4 marks available in total — a maximum of 2 marks each for points about the hacker and the council]

5 Points you might include:
  - The cinema should ask permission from the customer before storing their data.
  - The cinema should ask the customer to sign an agreement as to how the information should be used.
  - The cinema should only use the data to make it easier for customers to book seats and for contacting them for details on future films.
  - The cinema should give customers the option to unsubscribe from their service, so that their data is removed from the cinema's computer system if they want.
  - The cinema should be active in keeping its data up to date and allow their customers to change their details.
  - The cinema should not give customers' data to third party organisations unless the customer permits it.
  - The cinema should ensure that customers' data is held safely and securely, e.g. by using a firewall on its computer system and encrypting the data.

  How to mark your answer:
  - Two or three brief points with very little explanation. *[1-2 marks]*
  - Three or four detailed points that show a good understanding of the Data Protection Act. *[3-4 marks]*
  - Five or more detailed points that show a good understanding of the Data Protection Act and clearly apply it to the situation. *[5-6 marks]*

  Think about each principle of the Data Protection Act and apply it to this situation.

Pages 38-39: Mixed Questions

1 Points you might include:

  <u>Stakeholders</u>
  - Car and lorry drivers will receive benefits from having better, faster and shorter journeys.
  - Some residents on some routes will see an increase in traffic as they are used / recommended by satellite navigation systems.
  - Traditional printed map manufacturers may face loss of demand.
  - Satellite navigation system manufacturers will enjoy increased sales.

  <u>Technology</u>
  - Widespread use of satellite navigation devices will encourage the development of improvements, e.g. better options to customise routes, easier user interfaces, full speech recognition and wireless charging.
  - Standalone satellite navigation devices could become obsolete as more people use GPS and mapping applications on smartphones.

  <u>Ethical issues</u>
  - Potential for increased risk of accidents as devices are a distraction from driving, although may be better than printed maps.
  - Speed camera detection could encourage reckless driving as drivers can be safe in the knowledge they will be able to foresee speed cameras.

  <u>Environmental issues</u>
  - Widespread use of satellite navigation systems could result in shorter journey times, which means less overall fuel use and less pollution.
  - Satellite navigation devices require disposal when they break, and are less easy to recycle than paper maps.
  - Satellite navigation devices require electricity, which may come from non-renewable sources which cause pollution.
  - Satellite navigation devices may encourage people to make longer journeys by car rather than relying on public transport which could increase pollution.

  How to mark your answer:
  - Two or three brief points with very little explanation. *[1-2 marks]*
  - Three or four detailed points covering at least two of: stakeholders, technology, ethical issues and environmental issues *[3-4 marks]*
  - Five or more detailed points that form a well-written, balanced discussion, covering all of: stakeholders, technology, ethical issues and environmental issues. *[5-6 marks]*

2 Points you might include:

  <u>Technology</u>
  - The need to be able to contact anyone at any time on social media may increase the demand for smartphones and other mobile / wearable devices.
  - Software has adapted to suit social media needs. Many apps include 'share over social media' options. New social media apps and websites have been created in the hope of giving users (and advertisers) a new social media experience (e.g. Snapchat).

  <u>Ethical issues</u>
  - Social media increases the potential for cyberbullying and trolling, which could cause distress among its users.
  - Social media increases the potential for stalking and spying on others.
  - The significant time spent on social media means face-to-face interaction can be ignored.
  - The constant feedback and mental simulation gained from social media can be addictive for some people.

Answers

Privacy issues
- Social media encourages users to expand their online network of friends so that the social media company can gain new users and therefore more advertising revenue. This could affect people's privacy as they can share personal information with people they barely know.
- Social media tends to have lax security settings by default. This means the information people share on social media can often be viewed by those for which it was not intended.

Cultural issues
- Social media allows people with a range of different identities, opinions and backgrounds to communicate and share information with others. This allows people who don't normally get a voice to be heard, and allows other social media users to be exposed to a diverse range of views and experiences.
- Social media allows people with specific interests to more easily support causes they care about and meet like-minded people.
- Social media encourages users to post their views and photographs (including 'selfies') which contributes to a culture which might be becoming more self-centred and vain.

How to mark your answer:
- Two or three brief points with very little explanation. *[1-2 marks]*
- Three to five detailed points covering at least two of: technology, ethical issues, privacy issues and cultural issues. *[3-5 marks]*
- Six or more detailed points that form a well-written, balanced discussion, covering all of: technology, ethical issues, privacy issues and cultural issues. *[6-8 marks]*

3 Points you might include:

Stakeholders
- Manufacturers of notes and coins may lose out as their printing / minting services are less needed.
- Shopkeepers will have to invest in new technology to allow payment from phones.
- Users will always have a way of paying even if they forget their wallet.

Technology
- Mobile phones need to be designed with the appropriate hardware and software to make use of payment systems.
- Mobile phones need to have high quality security software to prevent theft and fraud.
- Mobile phones need to have a long battery life to ensure that people are not stranded without a way to make purchases.
- Mobile phone developers need to work with shops, banks and other retailers to make sure they have the technology to accept payments from mobile phones.

Ethical issues
- Transactions are easier on digital payment systems and the money is never visible. This may encourage people to spend more money, increasing the likelihood of them getting into debt.
- Digital payment may encourage more widespread hacking and computer misuse.

Environmental issues
- There is no need to dispose of old notes and coins, although e-waste caused by broken mobile devices arguably causes greater environmental damage.
- If digital payment systems become more popular, physical coins and notes may no longer be required and need to be disposed of.

How to mark your answer:
- Two or three brief points with very little explanation. *[1-2 marks]*
- Three or four detailed points covering at least two of: stakeholders, technology, ethical issues and environmental issues. *[3-4 marks]*
- Five or more detailed points that form a well-written, balanced discussion, covering all of: stakeholders, technology, ethical issues and environmental issues. *[5-6 marks]*

4 Points you might include:

Stakeholders
- Consumers will be able to access a greater variety of books, films and music. They will be able to purchase them at their own convenience without having to go to a shop. The books, films and music should also be cheaper as the costs are much lower to produce digital copies than physical copies.
- Traditional bookshops, CD shops and film retailers will have to adapt to distributing their stock digitally or face a decline in profits.
- Content creators will be able to distribute their media more cheaply, as they no longer have to pay for a record label, production team or publisher.
- New businesses that distribute books, music and films digitally could flourish as they gain some of the traditional stores' market share. New business models have been founded to distribute digital media, e.g. subscription-based services or streaming services where money is made through advertising.

Technology
- Use of digital media has encouraged the development and improvement in technology. E.g. e-readers introduced a new type of display technology that looks and feels more like a printed book. In the future, displays which are even more paper-like may be used.
- The use of digital media has placed extra demands on communication networks. This creates a cycle of improvement, e.g. watching high-quality films increases demand for better broadband speeds, which in turn encourages people to watch higher quality films, increasing demand for good broadband.
- The use of digital media is changing TVs from devices that receive broadcasted transmissions to Internet-enabled devices used to stream media from the Internet.

Environmental issues
- Less use of physical media means there could be less physical waste from packaging and discarded books, CDs and DVDs.
- No need for packaging or physical media, so fewer natural resources required in the distribution of the media.
- Greater use of digital media means increased use of electricity, as well as increased e-waste if hardware is discarded.

Legal issues
- Use of digital media could increase the amount of illegal file sharing.
- It is often unclear who owns the copyright to the original piece of work, and how profit from the book / music / film should be shared. E.g. how much money should a musician receive from their music being listened to on a free streaming service.
- It is often unclear who owns the digital file. E.g. should someone be able to pass their movie files onto their children, or does the ownership over them go back to the original distributor.

How to mark your answer:
- Two or three brief points with very little explanation. *[1-2 marks]*
- Three to five detailed points covering at least two of: stakeholders, technology, environmental issues and legal issues. *[3-5 marks]*
- Six or more detailed points that form a well-written, balanced discussion, covering all of: stakeholders, technology, environmental issues and legal issues. *[6-8 marks]*

100

Section Four — Algorithms

Page 40: Computational Thinking

Warm-Up

Decomposition is breaking down a complex problem into smaller problems and **solving** each one **individually**.
Abstraction is picking out the **important** bits of **information** from the problem, ignoring the specific **details** that don't matter.

1 a) Any **two** decomposition and matching abstraction processes. E.g.
- Decomposition: What will the keyboard look like? *[1 mark]* Abstraction: Ignore the colour and material. Focus on the layout and size. *[1 mark]*
- Decomposition: Which computers should it be compatible with? *[1 mark]* Abstraction: Ignore computers and operating systems more than 10 years old. Focus on newest and most common computers and operating systems. *[1 mark]*
- Decomposition: Are there any competitor keyboards? *[1 mark]* Abstraction: Ignore make and model names. Focus on price, features and quality. *[1 mark]*
[4 marks available in total]

b) Using logical steps to find a solution to a complex problem. *[1 mark]*

2 a) E.g. Abstraction is picking out important details and ignoring irrelevant ones. The file uploading service will focus on the important details like the file name and ignore the unimportant details like the contents of each file.
[3 marks available — 1 mark for a definition of abstraction, 1 mark for an example of a detail to ignore, 1 mark for an example of a detail to focus on]

b) E.g. Decomposition breaks the programming task down into smaller problems. A programmer might focus on 'How will the service keep track of files already uploaded?' or 'How will the service compare file names?' and try to solve each programming problem individually.
[3 marks available — 1 mark for a definition of decomposition, 1 mark for each example of decomposition up to a maximum of 2 marks]

Pages 41-43: Writing Algorithms

Warm-Up

| Input | Stop | Decision | Process |

1 a) An algorithm is a process or set of instructions used to solve a problem. *[1 mark]*

b) It asks the user to input a height and width as integers. *[1 mark]* It then multiplies these values together *[1 mark]* to get the area and prints the value of the area. *[1 mark]*

c) 5 × 10 = 50 *[1 mark]*

2 Asking for user input. *[1 mark]*
Comparing parcel number with requirement of eight characters. *[1 mark]*
Outputting "Valid parcel number." for correct cases. *[1 mark]*
Outputting "Not a valid parcel number." for invalid cases. *[1 mark]*
E.g.
parcelNumber = INPUT("Please enter your parcel number.")
IF parcelNumber has 8 characters THEN
    print("Valid parcel number")
ELSE
    print("Not a valid parcel number")
ENDIF

3 a) Any **one** problem, e.g.
- No Start / Begin box. *[1 mark]*
- No Stop / End box. *[1 mark]*
[1 mark available in total]

b) 10 * 8 ÷ 5 = 16 km *[1 mark]*

c) Using Start / Begin. *[1 mark]*
8/5 changed to 1.6093. *[1 mark]*
Decision box with appropriate question. *[1 mark]*
Creating a loop to input a new distance. *[1 mark]*
Using Stop / End. *[1 mark]*
E.g.

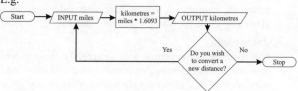

4 a) Decision box with appropriate question. *[1 mark]*
Output for winning ticket. *[1 mark]*
Output for losing ticket. *[1 mark]*
Using Stop / End. *[1 mark]*
E.g.

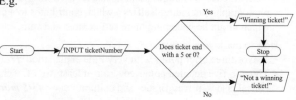

b) Using Start / Begin. *[1 mark]*
Using a counter to track number of tickets. *[1 mark]*
Using ticket subroutine appropriately. *[1 mark]*
Creating a loop that repeats 10 times. *[1 mark]*
Decision box with appropriate question. *[1 mark]*
Using Stop / End. *[1 mark]*
E.g.

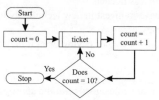

5 Using Start / Begin. *[1 mark]*
Asking user to input x, y. *[1 mark]*
Using SqMove (with correct subroutine box). *[1 mark]*
Decision box with appropriate question. *[1 mark]*
Creating a loop to repeat SqMove. *[1 mark]*
Using Stop / End. *[1 mark]*
E.g.

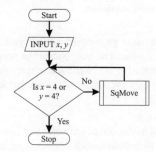

Answers

6 a) Using Start / Begin. *[1 mark]*
Decision boxes with appropriate questions. *[1 mark]*
Calculate discounts for existing customers correctly. *[1 mark]*
Calculate £5 off for costs ≥ £50 (new customers). *[1 mark]*
Arrows and Yes / No labels correctly drawn. *[1 mark]*
Using Stop / End. *[1 mark]*
E.g.

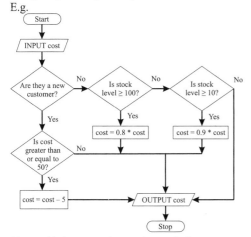

You could also use a decision box with three outcomes to check for each of the three possible stock levels.

b) Follow your flow diagram to find the cost, e.g.

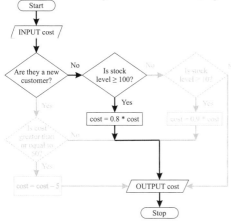

0.8 × £100 = £80 *[1 mark]*

Page 44: Search Algorithms

1 a) A binary search only works on ordered data. *[1 mark]*

b) Check the first item: 2 ≠ 13.
Check the second item: 3 ≠ 13.
Check the third item: 7 ≠ 13.
Check the fourth item: 5 ≠ 13.
Check the fifth item: 13 = 13.
Stop searching as the item has be found.
[2 marks available — 1 mark for starting with 2,
1 mark for checking items in order until you find 13]

2 a) Compare butterscotch to mint. *[1 mark]*
Mint is greater so split and take the left side. *[1 mark]*
A further comparison. *[1 mark]*
Correct identification of butterscotch. *[1 mark]*
E.g.
Middle item = (5 + 1) / 2 = 3rd item = mint.
Compare mint with butterscotch.
Butterscotch comes before mint, so take left hand side.
The list is: Butterscotch, Chocolate.
Middle item = (2 + 1) / 2 = 1.5 = 2nd item = chocolate.
Compare chocolate to butterscotch.
Butterscotch comes before chocolate, so take left hand side.
Middle item = (1 + 1) / 2 = 1st item = butterscotch.
Stop searching as butterscotch has been found.

b) It is much more efficient / takes fewer steps for large lists of items. *[1 mark]*
You won't get the mark for just saying it's quicker or more efficient.

c) There will be 11 items in total — so the middle item will be the (11 + 1) / 2 = 6th item. *[1 mark]*
The 9th item is after the 6th so take the right side. *[1 mark]*
This reduced list includes the 7th to 11th items of the original list — so 5 items in total.
Check the middle item which will the (5 + 1) / 2 = 3rd item of the reduced list (which is the 9th item of the original list).
It has taken 2 iterations to find the 9th item. *[1 mark]*

Pages 45-46: Sorting Algorithms

1

Riga	**Paris**	Oslo	Baku	Minsk
Paris	Riga	**Oslo**	Baku	Minsk
Oslo	Paris	Riga	**Baku**	Minsk
Baku	Oslo	Paris	Riga	**Minsk**
Baku	Minsk	Oslo	Paris	Riga

[4 marks available — 1 mark for each row from rows 2-5]

2 1st pass: 5 comparisons, 3 swaps.

5.32 m	**5.50 m**	5.39 m	6.50 m	6.28 m	6.14 m
5.32 m	**5.39 m**	**5.50 m**	6.50 m	6.28 m	6.14 m
5.32 m	5.39 m	**5.50 m**	**6.50 m**	6.28 m	6.14 m
5.32 m	5.39 m	5.50 m	**6.28 m**	**6.50 m**	6.14 m
5.32 m	5.39 m	5.50 m	6.28 m	**6.14 m**	**6.50 m**

2nd pass: 4 comparisons, 1 swap.

5.32 m	**5.39 m**	5.50 m	6.28 m	6.14 m	6.50 m
5.32 m	**5.39 m**	**5.50 m**	6.28 m	6.14 m	6.50 m
5.32 m	5.39 m	**5.50 m**	**6.28 m**	6.14 m	6.50 m
5.32 m	5.39 m	5.50 m	**6.14 m**	**6.28 m**	6.50 m

3rd pass: 3 comparisons, no swaps, list is ordered.

5.32 m	5.39 m	5.50 m	6.14 m	6.28 m	6.50 m

You can do multiple swaps in one stage but make it clear in your bubble sort if you do this.
[4 marks available — 1 mark for each correct swap,
1 mark for correct ordered list]

3 a) i)

3	**7**	6	2	5
7	3	**6**	2	5
7	6	3	**2**	5
7	6	3	2	**5**
7	6	5	3	2

[4 marks available — 1 mark for each row from rows 2-5]

ii) E.g.

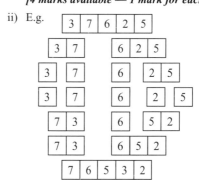

[4 marks available — 1 mark for correctly splitting the list into single items, 1 mark for each correct merging row]
The list doesn't split evenly so there is more than one way to get the right answer depending on how you split the items.

b) Any **one** benefit of insertion sort with contrast to merge sort, e.g.
- Insertion sort uses less memory *[1 mark]* as, unlike a merge sort, all the sorting is done on the original list. *[1 mark]*
- Insertion sort is quicker to check if a list is in order *[1 mark]* as a merge sort would still need to go through the splitting–merging process. *[1 mark]*
[2 marks available in total]

4 a) Compare 1989 and 1990 and don't swap.
Compare 1990 and 1992 and don't swap.
Compare 1992 and 1998 and don't swap.
Compare 1998 and 2000 and don't swap.
[2 marks for showing all correct comparisons, otherwise 1 mark for showing one correct comparison]

b) A bubble sort is efficient *[1 mark]* — for a list of *n* items you'd only need to do *n* – 1 comparisons. *[1 mark]*

5 a)

450	350	230	180	650	500	340	270

| 450 | 350 | 230 | 180 | | 650 | 500 | 340 | 270 |

| 450 | 350 | | 230 | 180 | | 650 | 500 | | 340 | 270 |

| 450 | | 350 | | 230 | | 180 | | 650 | | 500 | | 340 | | 270 |

| 350 | 450 | | 180 | 230 | | 500 | 650 | | 270 | 340 |

| 180 | 230 | 350 | 450 | | 270 | 340 | 500 | 650 |

| 180 | 230 | 270 | 340 | 350 | 450 | 500 | 650 |

[4 marks available — 1 mark for correctly splitting the list into single items, 1 mark for each correct merging row]

b) i) Small lists are easier to sort than larger lists. *[1 mark]*

ii) Ordered lists will be easier to merge at the next step of the algorithm. *[1 mark]*

Pages 47-48: Mixed Questions

1 a) Any **one** decomposition and matching abstraction process, e.g.
• Decomposition: Where is the tour? *[1 mark]*
  Abstraction: Ignore full venue address.
  Focus on the venue name and the city. *[1 mark]*
• What names should go on the advert? *[1 mark]*
  Ignore band members' names. Focus on the name of the band (and supporting bands). *[1 mark]*
• Where can tickets be bought? *[1 mark]*
  Ignore local retailers. Focus on ticket websites. *[1 mark]*
[2 marks available in total]

b) It would cost a basic user £5 + £1 = £6 and a premium user 5 × 0.5 = £2.50. *[1 mark]*
The difference is £6 – £2.50 = £3.50. *[1 mark]*

2 a) Check each item in order.
Check the first item: 10 mA ≠ 12 mA
Check the second item: 15 mA ≠ 12 mA
Check the third item: 12 mA = 12 mA.
Stop searching as the item has been found.
[2 marks available — 1 mark for starting with 10 mA, 1 mark for checking items in order until you find 12 mA]

b) Using Start / Begin. *[1 mark]*
Input to check reading. *[1 mark]*
Decision box with appropriate question. *[1 mark]*
'Buzz' as an output. *[1 mark]*
Wait 5 minutes as a process. *[1 mark]*
Using Stop / End. *[1 mark]*
E.g.

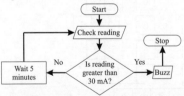

3 a) *Use abbreviations to reduce the size of the algorithm:*

Fl	Po	Ri	Va	Pa	Hi

| Fl | Po | Ri | | Va | Pa | Hi |

| Fl | Po | Ri | | Va | | Pa | Hi |

| Fl | Po | | Ri | | Va | Pa | Hi |

| Fl | Po | Ri | | Va | Hi | Pa |

| Fl | Po | Ri | | Hi | Pa | Va |

| Fl | Hi | Pa | Po | Ri | Va |

[4 marks available — 1 mark for correctly splitting the list into single items, 1 mark for each correct merging row]
The list doesn't split evenly so there is more than one way to get the right answer depending on how you split the items.

b) Compare Rings to Pommel. *[1 mark]*
Rings is greater so split and take the right side. *[1 mark]*
A further comparison. *[1 mark]*
Correct identification of Rings. *[1 mark]*
E.g.
Middle item = (6 + 1) / 2 = 3.5 = 4th item = Pommel.
Compare Pommel with Rings.
Rings is after Pommel, so take right hand side.
List becomes Rings, Vault
Middle item = (2 + 1) / 2 = 1.5 = 2nd item = Vault.
Rings is before Vault, so take left hand side.
List becomes Rings
Middle item = (1 + 1) / 2 = 1st item = Rings.
Stop searching as Rings has been found.

4 a) Using Start / Begin. *[1 mark]*
Input the outcome of two dice rolls. *[1 mark]*
Decision boxes with appropriate questions. *[1 mark]*
Calculating the score correctly and outputting it. *[1 mark]*
Arrows and Yes / No labels correctly drawn. *[1 mark]*
Using Stop / End. *[1 mark]*
E.g.

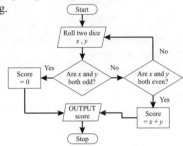

b) Linear Search *[1 mark]* — the list is unlikely to be ordered, so you couldn't use a binary search. *[1 mark]*

Section Five — Programming

Pages 49-50: Programming Basics

Warm-up

The number of people on a football pitch.
The age of a pet in whole months.
The number on a rolled dice.
The length of a car to the nearest metre.

1 Flavour — String *[1 mark]*
Weight (kg) — Real / Float *[1 mark]*
Quantity in stock — Integer *[1 mark]*
Gluten-Free? — Boolean *[1 mark]*

2 a) Takes the string "76423" and returns the integer 76423. *[1 mark]*

b) Returns the ASCII number for the character "T". *[1 mark]*

c) Returns the remainder when 12 is divided by 5, i.e. 2 *[1 mark]*

3 a) Boolean *[1 mark]* — the variable can only take two values, either pressed or not pressed, i.e. true or false. *[1 mark]*

b) Integer *[1 mark]* — it's measuring the number of whole seconds and whole numbers are best stored as integers. *[1 mark]*

4 a) z = x + y *[1 mark]*

b) z = x >= y *[1 mark]*

c) z = (x + y) / 160 * 100 *[1 mark]*

5 a) i) String *[1 mark]*

ii) Real / Float *[1 mark]*

b) Using the correct data type will make your programs more memory efficient. *[1 mark]* It will also make your programs more robust and predictable. *[1 mark]*

c) E.g. All the different data values might be converted to strings using the str() function so string concatenation can be used to join them together on the receipt. *[1 mark]* For example the cost of fuel might be converted from a real / float to a string so it can be printed in a sentence, e.g. "The cost of fuel was £20.76". *[1 mark]*

Page 51: Constants and Variables

1   a)   toppings *[1 mark]*
        eat_in *[1 mark]*

    b)   £1 *[1 mark]*

    c)   Any **two** reasons, e.g.
        • It doesn't need to be changed as the program is running.
          [1 mark]
        • Updating the value of a constant once will update it
          everywhere in the program. *[1 mark]*
        • It'll produce more meaningful code — a constant name of
          toppingsCost is clearer than 0.5. *[1 mark]*
        [2 marks available in total]

2   Investment is declared as a constant but its value changes. *[1 mark]*
    Interest is declared as an integer but it should take non-integer
    values. *[1 mark]*

3   E.g.
    Constant: An integer constant for the maximum number of
    customers allowed in the gym *[1 mark]* because it will never need
    to change. *[1 mark]*
    Variable 1: An integer variable for the current number of customers
    in the gym *[1 mark]* as the value will need to change whenever
    someone enters or leave the gym. *[1 mark]*
    Variable 2: A boolean variable to decide whether a card scan gains
    entry to the gym or not *[1 mark]* as the value will need to update
    every time a card is scanned. *[1 mark]*
    *Any appropriate constant / variable with a valid explanation will gain
    2 marks*

Page 52: Strings

Warm-up

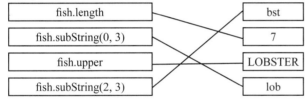

1   a)   14 *[1 mark]*

    b)   82016 *[1 mark]*

    c)   JAN *[1 mark]*

2   a)   Joining together two or more strings. *[1 mark]*

    b)   ORA2000 *[1 mark]*

    c)   05   fruit = fruit.upper *[1 mark]*
        06   prodID = fruit.subString(0, 3) *[1 mark]*
                    + str(volume) *[1 mark]*

Pages 53-55: Program Flow

Warm-up

    Selection Statements: IF-THEN-ELSE, SWITCH-CASE,
    IF-ELSEIF
    Iteration Statements: REPEAT-UNTIL, DO-UNTIL, WHILE

1   a)   Sequence *[1 mark]*

    b)   2 hours and 30 minutes *[1 mark]*

2   a)   Using an IF-ELSE or nested IF statement. *[1 mark]*
        Using the correct conditions to check all settings. *[1 mark]*
        Changing the temperature correctly for each setting. *[1 mark]*
        E.g.
        INT setting, temperature
        IF setting = = 3 THEN
           temperature = 50
        ELSEIF setting = = 2 THEN
           temperature = 30
        ELSEIF setting = = 1 THEN
           temperature = 20
        ELSE
           temperature = 0
        ENDIF

    b)   Any **two** reasons, e.g.
        • You only need to check the value of one variable. *[1 mark]*
        • The setting variable only has a set number of possible values.
          [1 mark]

3   a)   Declaring a variable as a string. *[1 mark]*
        Asking for an input from the user. *[1 mark]*
        Condition-controlled loop with appropriate condition. *[1 mark]*
        Appropriate feedback for a valid password. *[1 mark]*
        E.g.
        VAR password as STRING
        DO
           password = INPUT("Please enter a password")
        UNTIL password.length >=6
        print("Your password is valid")

    b)   E.g. The programmer might always want the code inside the
        loop to execute at least once. *[1 mark]*

4   a)   True and false *[1 mark]*

    b)   The player always gets the same number of shots. *[1 mark]*
        so you don't need to check a condition, just repeat the loop
        10 times. *[1 mark]*

    c)   Introduce a new variable that the user enters, e.g. shots
        [1 mark] and have the FOR loop go from 1 to this variable.
        E.g. FOR x = 1 to shots. *[1 mark]*

    d)   The game should check after every shot if the score is equal to
        5. *[1 mark]* A condition-controlled loop will keep repeating
        the game until the player has scored 5. *[1 mark]*

5   Using a condition controlled loop. *[1 mark]*
    Requesting an input from user for keypress. *[1 mark]*
    Concatenating keypress with the sentence. *[1 mark]*
    Using the correct terminating condition. *[1 mark]*
    Printing the sentence. *[1 mark]*
    E.g.
    CHAR keypress
    STRING sentence = ""
    DO
       INPUT keypress
       sentence = sentence + keypress
    UNTIL keypress = "." OR keypress = "?" OR keypress = "!"
    print(sentence)

6   Count controlled loop to allow 10 games. *[1 mark]*
    Asking for an input of the winner's name for each game. *[1 mark]*
    A selection statement for the winner of each game. *[1 mark]*
    Adding 1 to the winner's score. *[1 mark]*
    A selection statement to find the overall winner. *[1 mark]*
    Printing the correct message depending on the scores. *[1 mark]*
    E.g.
    INT karlWin = 0
    INT johnWin = 0
    STRING winner
    FOR i = 1 to 10
       winner = INPUT("Enter the winner's name")
       SWITCH winner:
          CASE "Karl":
             karlWin = karlWin + 1
          CASE "John":
             johnWin = johnWin + 1
       ENDSWITCH
    NEXT i
    IF karlWin > johnWin THEN
       print("The winner is Karl.")
    ELSEIF johnWin > karlWin THEN
       print("The winner is John.")
    ELSE
       print("The game is a draw.")
    ENDIF
    *To make your algorithm more robust you could have used input
    validation to make sure winner was either "Karl" or "John". You could
    also have named the variables differently so that the game could be
    played by any two players regardless of their name.*

Page 56: Boolean Operators

Warm-up

12 > 4 AND 5 == 5
12 <= 4 OR 10 != 5
NOT(11 == 3)
NOT(9 > 4 AND 5 < 2)

1 a) "Warning — Please alter the temperature." *[1 mark]*

b) "Warning — Please alter the humidity." *[1 mark]*

2 Using an appropriate selection statement. *[1 mark]*
A Boolean condition to check if the driver has paid
or has a permit. *[1 mark]*
Appropriate barrier conditions. *[1 mark]*
E.g.
BOOL barrierUp, ticketPaid, permitValid
Insert a ticket or permit
IF ticketPaid == true OR permitValid == true THEN
    barrierUp = true
ELSE
    barrierUp = false
ENDIF

3 Using an appropriate selection statement. *[1 mark]*
A Boolean condition that checks each of the conditions. *[1 mark]*
Allowing the dryer to start if conditions are met. *[1 mark]*
E.g.
REAL weight
BOOL allowStart, doorClosed
IF (weight > 1.5 AND weight < 15.0) AND doorClosed == true
THEN
    allowStart = true
ELSE
    allowStart = false
ENDIF

Page 57: File Handling

1 a) Line 01: Opens the file in read mode and stores it under the
variable myList. *[1 mark]*
Line 02: Prints the first line of the file, i.e. 1. Clean my room
[1 mark]
Line 03: Closes the file *[1 mark]*

b) The openWrite command will start writing from the start of the
file *[1 mark]* so the first line of the text file will be overwritten
with this text instead of it being added to the end. *[1 mark]*

2 Opening the story in read mode. *[1 mark]*
A condition-controlled loop to stop at the end of the file. *[1 mark]*
Waiting for a keypress input. *[1 mark]*
Using a selection statement to check the user's input. *[1 mark]*
Printing the next line of the story. *[1 mark]*
E.g.
CHAR keypress
story = openRead("adventure.txt")
WHILE NOT story.endOfFile()
  INPUT keypress
  IF keypress == "y" THEN
      print(story.readLine())
  ENDIF
ENDWHILE
story.close()

Pages 58-59: Storing Data

1 Text / String *[1 mark]*
Integer *[1 mark]*
Real / Float *[1 mark]*
Text / String *[1 mark]*
Boolean *[1 mark]*

2 a) 5 *[1 mark]*

b) A record is a row of the database used to store different pieces
of information for one entry (e.g. for a particular car). *[1 mark]*
A field is a column of the database used to store a particular
piece of information for every record (e.g. price of cars).
[1 mark]
*Just saying that records are rows and fields are columns will not be
awarded any marks without extra explanation.*

c) i)

Registration	Make
FQ55 ALW	Stanton
SQ57 TTW	Fenwick

[2 marks available — 1 mark for each correct record]

ii)

Make	Type
Stanton	Hatchback
Stanton	Saloon

[2 marks available — 1 mark for each correct record]

3 a) E.g. There is no unique field. *[1 mark]*

b) Any **two** reasons, e.g.
• Records separate data about different pupils. *[1 mark]*
• Records keep all data about a specific pupil together.
[1 mark]
• Records make retrieving data about pupils easier. *[1 mark]*
[2 marks available in total]

c) It will return all the records that are Year 10 pupils *[1 mark]*
and it will show every field. *[1 mark]*

4 a) i) ID Number *[1 mark]*

ii) Primary keys allow you to make sure that each record in
a table is unique. *[1 mark]* They can help to distinguish
between records. *[1 mark]* Primary keys make it easier to
retrieve or access specific records. *[1 mark]*
[2 marks available in total]

b) i) SELECT Title FROM comics
WHERE Genre = "Science Fiction"
*[2 marks available — 1 mark for selecting the correct
fields from the comics table, 1 mark for a correct 'where'
statement]*

ii) SELECT Title, Length FROM comics
WHERE Length < 50 AND Rating = 3
*[2 marks available — 1 mark for selecting the correct
fields from the comics table, 1 mark for a correct 'where'
statement]*

iii) SELECT * FROM comics WHERE Title LIKE "H%"
*[2 marks available — 1 mark for selecting all fields from
the comics table, 1 mark for a correct 'where' statement]*

Pages 60-61: Arrays

1 a) 440 500 *[1 mark]*

b) 510 000 – 429 000 = 81 000 *[1 mark]*

c) IF highscores[4] < newScore THEN
    Update the array.
ENDIF
*[2 marks available — 1 mark for using the element in
position 4 of the array, 1 mark for checking if the newScore is
greater than that element]*

2 a) Declaring five element array. *[1 mark]*
Assigning "Vanilla" to position 0. *[1 mark]*
All remaining elements in the correct position. *[1 mark]*
E.g.
ARRAY cupcakes[5]
cupcakes[0] = "Vanilla"
cupcakes[1] = "Banana"
cupcakes[2] = "Strawberry"
cupcakes[3] = "Cherry"
cupcakes[4] = "Caramel"
Don't forget to use " " as you're dealing with strings.

b) print(cupcakes[0]) *[1 mark]*

c) cupcakes[3] = "Raspberry" *[1 mark]*

3 a) String *[1 mark]*

b) Any **three** reasons, e.g.
- Multiple items of data need to be stored. *[1 mark]*
- All the data being stored has the same data type. *[1 mark]*
- The data is split by two categories / can be represented in a table so a 2D array is useful for storing it. *[1 mark]*
- Stores the data together under one variable name. *[1 mark]*
- Accessing the information is more efficient. A single command, e.g. *sportsDay[position, event]* can be used to access any name from the array. *[1 mark]*

[3 marks available in total — at least one reason must specifically mention 2D arrays.]

4 a) print(distanceRun[4, 3]) *[1 mark]*

b) Asking the user to input the runner number. *[1 mark]*
Using a FOR loop. *[1 mark]*
Adding all elements correctly. *[1 mark]*
Printing the total distance. *[1 mark]*
E.g.
```
INT totalDistance = 0
INT runner
runner = INPUT("Choose a runner number from 0-3")
FOR i = 0 to 6
    totalDistance = totalDistance + distanceRun[i, runner]
NEXT i
print(totalDistance)
```

c) A FOR loop going from 0 to 3. *[1 mark]*
A FOR loop going from 0 to 6. *[1 mark]*
Using milesConvert() on each element of the array. *[1 mark]*
E.g.
```
FOR i = 0 to 3
    FOR j = 0 to 6
        distanceRun[i, j] = milesConvert(distanceRun[i, j])
    NEXT j
NEXT i
```

Pages 62-63: Sub Programs

1 A function that takes an integer as a parameter. *[1 mark]*
Finding the cube and square of the integer. *[1 mark]*
Returning the difference between the cube and square. *[1 mark]*
E.g.
```
FUNCTION cubeSquare(num as INT) as INT
    return(num^3 – num^2)
ENDFUNCTION
```

2 a) Any **three** benefits, e.g.
- She will only have to write them once so she doesn't have to repeat blocks of code. *[1 mark]*
- She can call them from anywhere in the program. *[1 mark]*
- She only has to debug them once. *[1 mark]*
- They will improve the readability / maintainability of her code. *[1 mark]*
- They break the program down into smaller more manageable chunks. *[1 mark]*

[3 marks available in total]

b) A function will return a value, a procedure will not. *[1 mark]*

3 a) Any **two** differences, e.g.
- Local variables can only be changed and accessed from within the part of the program they're declared in. *[1 mark]* Global variables can be changed and accessed from anywhere in the program. *[1 mark]*
- The same local variable name can be used in different sub programs and declared differently each time. *[1 mark]* Global variable names can only be declared once. *[1 mark]*
- Local variables are declared inside part of a program (e.g. in a sub program). *[1 mark]* Global variables are usually declared at the start of the main program. *[1 mark]*

[4 marks available in total]

b) A function that takes the number of sides the dice have as a parameter. *[1 mark]*
Using a condition controlled loop. *[1 mark]*
Simulating two dice rolls. *[1 mark]*
Increasing the score by 1 after each roll. *[1 mark]*
Returning the score. *[1 mark]*
E.g.
```
FUNCTION rollDouble(side as INT) as INT
    INT score = 0
    INT x, y
    DO
        x = roll(side)
        y = roll(side)
        score = score + 1
    UNTIL x == y
    return(score)
ENDFUNCTION
```

4 a) i) A parameter is a special variable that passes data into a sub program. *[1 mark]*

ii) Parameters have a local scope to the sub program they're defined in. *[1 mark]*

iii) Arguments are the actual values that parameters take when the sub program is called. *[1 mark]*

b) i) Declares a new integer variable, difficulty, *[1 mark]* which has global scope so it can be used anywhere in the program. *[1 mark]*

ii) It takes weight as a parameter *[1 mark]* and sets the initial difficulty to the integer (quotient) part when weight is divided by 6. *[1 mark]*

c) A sub program that takes heart rate as a parameter. *[1 mark]*
Using a selection statement. *[1 mark]*
Having correct conditions on the selection statement. *[1 mark]*
Setting the difficulty depending on the conditions. *[1 mark]*
E.g.
```
PROCEDURE adjustLevel(heartrate as INT)
    IF heartrate > 160
        difficulty = 0
        print("Slow Down!")
    ELSEIF heartrate < 90
        difficulty = difficulty + 1
    ELSEIF heartrate > 140
        difficulty = difficulty – 1
    ENDIF
ENDPROCEDURE
```

Pages 64-65: Mixed Questions

1 a) String *[1 mark]*
Integer *[1 mark]*

b) Using a selection statement. *[1 mark]*
Using the correct conditions. *[1 mark]*
Altering the power depending on the condition. *[1 mark]*
Printing the setting and power correctly. *[1 mark]*
E.g.
```
STRING setting
INT power
SWITCH setting:
    CASE "Defrost":
        power = 200
    CASE "Medium":
        power = 650
    CASE "High":
        power = 900
ENDSWITCH
print(setting + " " + str(power) + "W")
```

2 a) 55.0 *[1 mark]*
Answer must be given as real / float.

b) Declaring a procedure that takes the new average speed as a parameter. *[1 mark]*
Using an appropriate iteration statement. *[1 mark]*
Moving the elements in the array to the next position. *[1 mark]*
Updating position 0 of the array with the new average speed. *[1 mark]*
E.g.
PROCEDURE updateSpeeds(newSpeed as REAL)
  FOR i = 9 to 1
    journeySpeeds[i] = journeySpeeds[i-1]
  NEXT i
  journeySpeeds[0] = newSpeed
ENDPROCEDURE
Hint: Remember that the last element of the array is in position 9, not position 10.

3 a) ARRAY primeKoalas[4, 2]
primeKoalas[0, 0] = "John"
primeKoalas[1, 0] = "Paul"
primeKoalas[2, 0] = "Cheryl"
primeKoalas[3, 0] = "Ida"
primeKoalas[0, 1] = "guitar"
primeKoalas[1, 1] = "bass"
primeKoalas[2, 1] = "vocals"
primeKoalas[3, 1] = "drums"
[2 marks available — 2 marks for all 4 correct lines of code, otherwise 1 mark for at least two correct lines of code]

b) Opening and closing the file properly. *[1 mark]*
Using a loop. *[1 mark]*
Writing the name and instrument of each band member to the file. *[1 mark]*
E.g.
band = openWrite("musicians.txt")
FOR i = 0 to 3
  band.writeLine(primeKoalas[i, 0] + " " + primeKoalas[i, 1])
NEXT i
band.close()

c) Any **two** advantages with explanations, e.g.
• Text files don't lose data when the program stops. *[1 mark]* So the program can pick up where it left off the next time it runs. *[1 mark]*
• Text files can be accessed at any time. *[1 mark]* So data can be read from or written to them even when the program isn't running. *[1 mark]*
• Text files give you more flexibility over what you can store. *[1 mark]* You don't need to worry about data types or how they are structured. *[1 mark]*
[4 marks available in total]

d) A procedure taking a file name as a parameter. *[1 mark]*
Opening the file in read mode. *[1 mark]*
A condition-controlled loop to stop at the end of the file. *[1 mark]*
Using the toSpeech() procedure to read out each line. *[1 mark]*
Closing the file. *[1 mark]*
E.g.
PROCEDURE readAll(fileName as STRING)
  file = openRead(fileName)
  WHILE NOT file.endOfFile()
    toSpeech(file.readLine())
  ENDWHILE
  file.close()
ENDPROCEDURE
It's important that you always remember to close a file once you're finished reading from it or writing to it.

Section Six — Design, Testing and IDEs

Pages 66-67: Defensive Design

1 a) Checking data meets certain criteria before passing it into the program or database. *[1 mark]*

b) Any **two** suitable input validations, e.g.
• Check that the input value is an integer. *[1 mark]*
• Check that the input value is positive. *[1 mark]*
• Check that the input value is within the range of possible ages, e.g. less than 120. *[1 mark]*
[2 marks available in total]

c) Any **two** suitable input validations, e.g.
• Check that the string contains only letters and numbers. *[1 mark]*
• Check that the postcode is the correct length. *[1 mark]*
• Check that the postcode has the correct form, e.g. always ends with a number then two letters. *[1 mark]*
[2 marks available in total]

2 E.g.
• Indentation can improve readability by showing where different statements start and finish *[1 mark]* e.g. Jessica could indent within the IF / ELSE statement. *[1 mark]*
• Comments can be used to help explain the code *[1 mark]* e.g. on line 6 Jessica could include the comment // checks whether the base input is valid. *[1 mark]*
• Variable names can be used to make it easier to identify what the variables do *[1 mark]* e.g. Jessica could have given the variables 'num1' and 'num2' names like 'area' and 'base'. *[1 mark]*

3 a) A means of confirming the identity of a user before they can access a program or part of a program. *[1 mark]*

b) E.g.
• The program deals with extremely sensitive personal data *[1 mark]* so it is important that information cannot be stolen or accessed by the wrong people. *[1 mark]*
• Different types of hospital staff may need to access the records *[1 mark]* so it will allow these different users access to the exact information they need and nothing more. *[1 mark]*
[2 marks available in total]

c) E.g. too much authentication can affect a program's functionality and put people off using it. *[1 mark]*

4 a) Any **two** ways with valid explanations, e.g.
• Agreeing how and when to use comments will improve the maintainability *[1 mark]* as the team will be able to understand each other's code. *[1 mark]*
• Agreeing how and when to use global variables will lead to fewer errors *[1 mark]* as each person's code is more likely to work with the other developers' code. *[1 mark]*
• Agreeing how to validate and sanitise inputs will reduce errors *[1 mark]* as all parts of the program will accept similar inputs. *[1 mark]*
[4 marks available in total]

b) E.g. Malcolm could use input sanitisation *[1 mark]* with the space character being removed when the flight number is input into the program. *[1 mark]*

5 E.g.
• Input validation could make sure that only appropriate data was entered. *[1 mark]* E.g. only allowing numbers to be entered for the card number. *[1 mark]*
• Input validation would ensure the input data matches certain criteria or is of a certain format. *[1 mark]* E.g. it can make sure that the expiration month is between 1 and 12. *[1 mark]*
• Input validation alone will not prevent all errors. *[1 mark]* E.g. it cannot check that a customer's card number matches their name. *[1 mark]*
• Using input sanitisation alongside validation would improve the defensive design *[1 mark]* as you'd be able to remove unwanted parts of an input before validating it. *[1 mark]*
[6 marks available in total]

Pages 68-69: Testing

Warm-up

The statements that should be ticked are:
Using the wrong boolean operator is a logic error.
Syntax errors will prevent code from running.

1   a)   A type of error caused by the code not following the rules or grammar of the programming language. *[1 mark]*

   b)   The code will translate and run *[1 mark]* but it will not behave as Huey intended. *[1 mark]*

2   a)   Error: Missing bracket on line 4. *[1 mark]*
      Correction: print("Valid pincode") *[1 mark]*

   b)   Error: Wrong Boolean operator in line 3. *[1 mark]*
      Correction: IF pincode.length >= 4 AND pincode.length <= 6 THEN *[1 mark]*
      Tiffany's code currently allows any pincode length. Changing OR to AND makes sure only pincodes with lengths from 4 to 6 characters are allowed.

3   a)   E.g. a test plan should take the user down all possible paths of the program. *[1 mark]* It should use normal, extreme and erroneous test data. *[1 mark]* If any of the tests get a result not equal to the expected outcome then the user knows there is a logic error. *[1 mark]*

   b)

Test Data	Expected Outcome	Reasons for test
Group_Size = 4	210	Check program with data user is likely to input.
Group_Size = 9	460	Check program works with values on the limit.
Group_Size = 12	Display an error message	Check what happens if input is too large.

[5 marks available — 1 mark per box]

4   a)   i)   The program is only tested once *[1 mark]* and is signed off if it meets the initial requirements. *[1 mark]*

       ii) The program goes through several development cycles *[1 mark]* in which the program is tested and the requirements adjusted. *[1 mark]*

   b)   Any **one** advantage with explanation, e.g.
      • Final testing is a much quicker process than iterative testing *[1 mark]* so the program can be completed sooner. *[1 mark]*

      Any **one** disadvantage with explanation, e.g.
      • Final testing may produce an inferior program *[1 mark]* because there is no opportunity to improve the program based on feedback from the customer or users. *[1 mark]*
      • Final testing is unlikely to allow the developer to include more features *[1 mark]* because the requirements cannot be adjusted. *[1 mark]*
      [4 marks available in total]

Page 70: Translators

1   An interpreter *[1 mark]* translates the code as the program is running, one instruction at a time. *[1 mark]*
A compiler *[1 mark]* translates all the source code in one go and creates an executable file. *[1 mark]*

2   a)   Any **two** reasons, e.g.
      • They may need to have a greater control over the program in order to make a program with lower memory use. *[1 mark]*
      • They may need to have a greater control over what the CPU does in order to make a program run quicker. *[1 mark]*
      • They may be trying to maintain old code or hardware. *[1 mark]*
      [2 marks available in total]

   b)   Assembly languages are more readable for humans than machine code *[1 mark]* so can be programmed / edited more easily. *[1 mark]*

   c)   Assembler *[1 mark]*

3   Any **three** differences, e.g.
   • One instruction of high-level code represents many instructions of machine code, *[1 mark]* whereas one instruction of low-level code often represents one instruction of machine code. *[1 mark]*
   • High-level code works for many different machines and processors, *[1 mark]* whereas low-level languages normally only work for one type of machine or processor. *[1 mark]*
   • A programmer using a high-level language can easily store data without knowing about the memory structure, *[1 mark]* whereas a programmer using a low-level language needs to know how the CPU manages the memory. *[1 mark]*
   • Code written in a high-level language is easy for other programmers to understand and modify, *[1 mark]* whereas it is more difficult for other programmers to understand and modify code written in a low-level languages. *[1 mark]*
   [6 marks available in total]

Page 71: Integrated Development Environments

Warm-up

Code Editor: used for writing code.

Breakpoints: a debugging tool that stops the program at certain points.

Error Diagnostics: highlight errors in the program.

1   a)   A translator turns the source code into machine code *[1 mark]* allowing Cynthia to run the application. *[1 mark]*
      Error Diagnostics highlight errors in the code *[1 mark]* allowing Cynthia to easily find and fix errors in her application. *[1 mark]*
      A Code editor allows the user to enter code and includes features like indenting, auto-correct, line numbering and colour coding *[1 mark]* making it a lot easier for Cynthia to write and maintain her application. *[1 mark]*

   b)   The translator will pick up syntax errors as it will be unable to translate the code. *[1 mark]* These errors along with their location will be shown in the error diagnostics panel. *[1 mark]* The code editor lets Cynthia navigate to the correct line and correct the error. *[1 mark]*

2   E.g.
   • Run-time environment runs the program within the IDE *[1 mark]* so Max can see which part of the code is running when the logic errors occur. *[1 mark]*
   • Breakpoints allow Max to stop the program on certain lines as the program is running *[1 mark]* allowing Max to gather information about the values of particular variables. *[1 mark]*
   • Error diagnostics will alert Max to possible errors, e.g. using the wrong data type *[1 mark]* which may be causing logic errors even though it is not breaking the language syntax. *[1 mark]*
   [4 marks available in total]

Pages 72-73: Mixed Questions

1   a)   Erroneous test data contains values that the program should not accept. *[1 mark]* Using them in testing will make sure that the user can enter any data without breaking the program. *[1 mark]*

   b)   i)   Type of data: Normal *[1 mark]*
         Expected Outcome: 20 *[1 mark]*
         Actual Outcome: 20 *[1 mark]*

       ii) Type of data: Erroneous *[1 mark]*
         Expected Outcome: User receives an error message, e.g. "Invalid dice score, please re-enter." *[1 mark]*
         Actual Outcome: 19 *[1 mark]*
         The game uses a six-sided dice, so if the user inputs a 9 they should receive an error message. However, Tony's program

does not check for this.

c) Any **one** way, e.g.
- Tony can use input validation to make sure only integers are accepted. *[1 mark]*
- Tony can use input validation to make sure only the numbers from 1 to 6 are accepted (he can use a whitelist to do this). *[1 mark]*
- Tony can use input validation to ensure that the input is only one character long. *[1 mark]*

[2 marks available in total]

2 a) Logic error: FOR x = 0 to 10 *[1 mark]*
Explanation: The email address may be longer than eleven characters. *[1 mark]*

b) Comments *[1 mark]* would explain aspects of the code so they are understood by other developers. *[1 mark]*
This is the only possible answer because Natasha's code uses indentation and clearly named variables already.

c) Any **one** way with an explanation, e.g.
- Most email addresses end in a similar way. *[1 mark]* Use a whitelist to check that the ending is valid, for example, .co.uk or .com. *[1 mark]*
- Check the email address contains a '.' character *[1 mark]* as most email addresses will contain a full stop. *[1 mark]*

[2 marks available in total]

d) Any **two** ways, E.g.
- A compiler would produce an executable file *[1 mark]* while an interpreter would not. *[1 mark]*
- A compiler would list any errors at the end of the translation *[1 mark]* while an interpreter would return the first error it found then stop. *[1 mark]*
- A compiler would translate the code all at once *[1 mark]* while an interpreter would translate the code line by line. *[1 mark]*

[4 marks available in total]

3 E.g.
- The code editor might include an auto-indentation feature *[1 mark]* which will make the code clearer to read. *[1 mark]*
- The code editor might include an auto-colour feature *[1 mark]* which makes it easier to distinguish between different features of the code, e.g. variables and comments. *[1 mark]*
- Finding logic errors requires a lot of work by the user — the IDE has debugging tools to help *[1 mark]* but most of the work is done through testing. *[1 mark]*
- The IDE won't be able to tell if clear variable names and comments have been used *[1 mark]* so it won't be able to help with this, it's up to the developer. *[1 mark]*
- The IDE can't check if programmers have used a consistent approach in different parts of the program *[1 mark]* so it will be up to the developers to maintain good practice. *[1 mark]*

[6 marks available in total]

Section Seven — Data Representation

Pages 74-75: Logic

1 a)
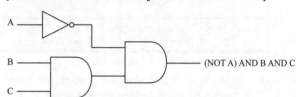
A —[NOT]— P *[1 mark]*

b)
A, B —[OR]— Q *[1 mark]*

2 a) B = 0 *[1 mark]*

b) A = 1, B = 1 *[1 mark]*
A and B must both be 1 for the output of an AND gate to be 1. The NOT gate changes the 1 to a 0.

3 a)

A	B	Q
FALSE	FALSE	TRUE
FALSE	TRUE	FALSE
TRUE	FALSE	TRUE
TRUE	TRUE	TRUE

[3 marks available — 1 mark for each correct row]

b) The NOT logic gate is pointing the wrong way. *[1 mark]*
The OR gate should only have one output. *[1 mark]*

4 a)

A	B	C	NOT A	B AND C	(NOT A) AND (B AND C)
0	0	0	1	0	0
0	0	1	1	0	0
0	1	0	1	0	0
0	1	1	1	1	1
1	0	0	0	0	0
1	0	1	0	0	0
1	1	0	0	0	0
1	1	1	0	1	0

[3 marks available — 1 mark for each correct column]

b)
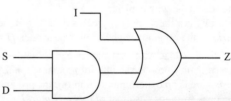
(NOT A) AND B AND C

[3 marks available — 1 mark for input A going into a NOT gate, 1 mark for inputs B and C going into an AND gate, 1 mark for outputs going into an AND gate with one output]

5 a)

[3 marks available — 1 mark for inputs S and D going into an AND gate, 1 mark for the output of AND gate and input I going into an OR gate, 1 mark for Z being the OR gate output]

b) (S AND D) OR I = Z *[1 mark]*

c) i) S = 0, D = 1, I = 0, Z = 0 *[1 mark]*

ii) S = 1, D = 1, I = 1, Z = 1 *[1 mark]*
S = 1, D = 0, I = 1, Z = 1 *[1 mark]*

Page 76: Units

Warm-up

Bit, Nibble, Byte, Kilobyte, Petabyte

1 a) 0.3 Terabyte *[1 mark]*
1 TB = 1000 GB, 1 GB = 1000 MB. 0.3 TB = 300 GB and 200 000 MB = 200 GB, so 0.3 TB is the largest.

b) 1 GB = 1000 MB
250 GB = 250 000 MB *[1 mark]*
250 000 MB ÷ 5 MB = 50 000 *[1 mark]*

2 a) A digit added to the end of a string of numbers / data to check that data has been entered and received correctly. *[1 mark]* The value is calculated from the digits in the string. *[1 mark]*

b) Computers are made up of logic circuits *[1 mark]* which use 1 and 0 to show high and low voltage. *[1 mark]*

c) String 1 contains an error *[1 mark]* because it has an odd number of 1s. *[1 mark]*

d) In the case where an even number of bits are read incorrectly *[1 mark]* a parity bit will not detect an error. *[1 mark]*

Pages 77-78: Binary Numbers

Warm-up

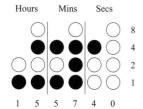

1 a) 147 *[1 mark]*

b) 11111100 *[1 mark]*
Draw up a table to help with binary addition and conversions.

2 a)
```
   0 0 1 1 1 0 0 1
+  0 1 0 1 0 1 1 0
   ---------------
   1 0 0 0 1 1 1 1
   1 1 1
```
[2 marks available — 1 mark for correct working, 1 mark for correct answer]

b) i) Two suitable binary numbers which, when added, will cause overflow. *[1 mark]* Correct addition of the chosen binary numbers. *[1 mark]* E.g. 11111111 + 00000001 = 100000000 (9 bits)

ii) The computer would flag up the error *[1 mark]* and usually store the extra bits elsewhere. *[1 mark]*

3 a) 11010000 *[1 mark]*

b) A 2 place right shift *[1 mark]* gives 00110101. *[1 mark]*

c) Ife is not correct. E.g. 0001 + 0001 = 0010 is a 1 place left shift. *[2 marks available — 1 mark for not correct, 1 mark for a valid explanation]*

4 a) 128 *[1 mark]*
8-bit means there are 2^8 = 256 possibilities but only half of them are magic words.

b) 01010000 + 01100110 = 10110110. *[1 mark]* Changing the last digit to a 1 gives 10110111 which is the Blizzard spell. *[1 mark]*

c) Shazam and Pocus 00110100 + 11001010 = 11111110. Changing the last digit gives 11111111, the Earthquake spell. *[2 marks available — 1 mark for the correct answers, 1 mark for showing correct working]*
The first seven digits of Shazam and Pocus have 0s and 1s in opposite places, so you can quickly work out that these add to a binary number of all 1s.

Pages 79-80: Hexadecimal Numbers

Warm-up

A + **2** = C,   6 + **8** = E,   **6** + 6 = C,   F + **F** = 1E

1 a) 255 *[1 mark]*
FF = (16 × 15) + 15 = 255 in denary.

b) 3 × 16 = 48 *[1 mark]*
48 + 7 = 55 *[1 mark]*

c) 45 ÷ 16 = 2 r 13. *[1 mark]* 13 is the remainder which is D in hex. So 45 is 2D in hex. *[1 mark]*

2 a) Split bytes into nibbles and convert to hexadecimal. 0100 = 4, 0011 = 3, so 01000011 = C = 43. *[1 mark]* 0100 = 4, 0001 = 1, so 01000001 = A = 41. *[1 mark]* 0101 = 5, 0100 = 4, so 01010100 = T = 54. *[1 mark]*

b) i) D = 44 = 01000100 *[1 mark]*

ii) From CAT, 43 = C and from DOG, 44 = D and 4F = O. E is 1 more than D (= 44) so 45 = E. *[1 mark]* The password is CODE. *[1 mark]*

3 Convert each hex number to denary: 10 = (1 × 16) = 16, 25 = (2 × 16) + 5 = 37, 3A = (3 × 16) + A (= 10) = 58. Adding the denary numbers together gives 16 + 37 + 58 = 111. On the right hand side, convert 6F to denary: (6 × 16) + 15 = 96 + 15 = 111. Both sides equal 111, so the equation is correct. *[4 marks available — 1 mark for converting any hexadecimal to denary, 1 mark for converting all hexadecimals on left hand side to denary, 1 mark for left hand side adding to 111, 1 mark for showing that right hand side also equals 111]*

4 E.g.
They would likely agree with claim 1. *[1 mark]*
Hex numbers are shorter so are easier to identify, remember, edit and share than binary codes. *[1 mark]*
They would likely disagree with claim 2. *[1 mark]*
Converting binary to hex is easier than denary to hex — binary numbers can be split into nibbles to quickly read off the hex values. *[1 mark]*

5 a) denary(A) = 10 and denary(C) = 12 *[1 mark]*
So, denary(A) + denary(C) = 10 + 12 = 22 *[1 mark]*

b) Taking a hexadecimal as an input. *[1 mark]*
Splitting hexadecimal into characters. *[1 mark]*
Multiplying first character in denary by 16. *[1 mark]*
Adding the second character in denary to the first. *[1 mark]*
E.g.
```
hexadecimal = INPUT("Enter a two digit hexadecimal")
char1 = hexadecimal[0]
char2 = hexadecimal[1]
ans = 16 * denary(char1) + denary(char2)
print(ans)
```

Page 81: Characters

1 a) A character set is a collection of characters a computer recognises from their binary representation. *[1 mark]*

b) Binary code sent to computer. *[1 mark]*
Character set used to translate binary code. *[1 mark]*

2 a) i) In general using more bits to represent characters increases the size of the character set. *[1 mark]*

ii) E.g.
• All ASCII characters start with a 0. *[1 mark]*
• ASCII is really a 7-bit character set. *[1 mark]*
• Extended ASCII has 2^8 unique characters (256) but ASCII has 2^7 unique characters (128). *[1 mark]*
[2 marks available in total]

iii) He is incorrect. *[1 mark]* UTF-32 could represent 2^{32} characters which is much more than 4 × 2^8. *[1 mark]*

b) Any **two** benefits, e.g.
• It can support a large number of characters. *[1 mark]*
• Can use the same character set to type in lots of different languages. *[1 mark]*
• Easier for systems to operate globally. *[1 mark]*
[2 marks available in total]

110

Page 82: Storing Images

1 a) The number of bits per pixel determines the number of possible colours *[1 mark]* and so increases the amount of unique colours an image has available to use. *[1 mark]*

b) $256 = 2^8$, so 8 bits per pixel are needed. *[1 mark]*

c) In image 1, 1 bit is needed to represent each pixel (black or white) and there are 15 pixels. $15 \times 1 = 15$ bits. *[1 mark]*
In image 2, 2 bits are needed to represent each pixel (4 different colours) and there are 9 pixels. $9 \times 2 = 18$ bits. *[1 mark]*
In image 3, 1 bit is needed to represent each pixel and there are 16 pixels. $16 \times 1 = 16$ bits. *[1 mark]*
So image 2 requires the most bits to represent it. *[1 mark]*

2 a) i) The number of pixels per unit length / area (normally measured in DPI). *[1 mark]*

ii) $60 \times 60 \times 10 \times 10$ *[1 mark]* $= 360\,000$ *[1 mark]*

b) A lower DPI would reduce the quality of the image *[1 mark]* because the number of pixels in a given area decreases. *[1 mark]*

c) Metadata is 'data about data' / information about a file. *[1 mark]* Metadata includes information about height, width, resolution etc. so the image is displayed properly. *[1 mark]*

Page 83: Storing Sound

1 a)

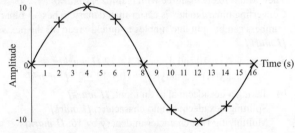

[1 mark for a correct diagram]

b) E.g.
INPUT analogue sound. *[1 mark]*
Samples taken of amplitude at specific intervals. *[1 mark]*
Samples turned into binary / digital data. *[1 mark]*
OUTPUT digital data. *[1 mark]*

2 a) Extract 2 would have a better sound quality *[1 mark]* because it has a larger bit rate and sampling frequency, both of which are indications of better overall sound quality. *[1 mark]*

b) The file size would be larger. *[1 mark]*

Page 84: Compression

1 a) Audio files can be very large especially for long podcasts. Compression is used to reduce the overall size of the audio file *[1 mark]* with some acceptable loss of quality. *[1 mark]*

b) Any **one** benefit, e.g.
• It will be higher quality.
• It will match the original digital sample exactly.

Any **one** drawback, e.g.
• The file size will be bigger.
• It will take longer to download.
[2 marks available in total — 1 mark for a correct benefit, 1 mark for a correct drawback]

c) Any **two** reasons with explanations, e.g.
• The MP3 file will be smaller than the FLAC file *[1 mark]* and she may not have enough storage space on her smartphone for the FLAC file. *[1 mark]*
• The MP3 file will be smaller *[1 mark]* so it would be quicker to download if her Internet connection is slow. *[1 mark]*
• Not all media players support all file types. *[1 mark]* The media player on her smartphone may not support FLAC files. *[1 mark]*
[4 marks available in total]

2 a) Any **one** compression type and relevant explanation, e.g.
• Lossy compression *[1 mark]* — uploading is quicker as the file sizes are reduced. *[1 mark]*
• Lossless compression *[1 mark]* — she may want to share high quality images with friends / colleagues. *[1 mark]*
[2 marks available in total]

b) Any **one** compression type and relevant explanation, e.g.
• Lossy compression *[1 mark]* — a high quality JPEG file may have sufficient quality. *[1 mark]*
• Lossless compression *[1 mark]* — an image with all original detail may be preferred so they can edit it and print it at the best possible resolution. *[1 mark]*
[2 marks available in total]

Pages 85-86: Mixed Questions

1 a) A 2 place left shift on 10010110 is 01011000. *[1 mark]*
Convert 01011000 to hex by splitting into nibbles:
0101 is 5 in hex, and 1000 is 8. *[1 mark]*
So 01011000 is 58 as a hexadecimal. *[1 mark]*

b) Split 2 and C and work out the binary conversion:
2 is 0010 *[1 mark]* and C = 12 = 1100. *[1 mark]*
So 2C is 00101100.
A 2 place right shift on 00101100 is 00001011. *[1 mark]*
01001011, 10001011 and 11001011 are equally valid.

2 a) Denary Value = 200 *[1 mark]*
Binary Value = 11001000 *[1 mark]*
Hex Value = C8 *[1 mark]*

b) Decreasing the sampling interval means that more samples are taken every second. *[1 mark]* The sound quality will be better as the file will more closely match the original. *[1 mark]*

c) The radio broadcast is three hours long so the size of the file will likely be quite large. *[1 mark]* Lossy compression would greatly reduce the size of the file and the change in sound quality would be barely noticeable. *[1 mark]*

3 a) i) 01001101 *[1 mark]*
M is 2 letters away from K so to find the binary representation of M, add 2 (in binary) to K, i.e. 01001011 + 00000010.

ii) P = 01010000 in binary. *[1 mark]*
Split into nibbles: 0101 is 5 and 0000 is 0 in binary.
So P is 50 as a hexadecimal. *[1 mark]*
P is 5 letters away from K so to find the binary representation of P, add 5 (in binary) to K, i.e. 01001011 + 00000101.

b) The Unicode representation will tend to be longer. *[1 mark]*

4 a) 16^6 *[1 mark]*

b) E.g. It would be easier to remember the hex code for a particular colour *[1 mark]* because the hex code would be shorter than the binary or denary equivalents. *[1 mark]*

c) JPEG is an example of lossy compression *[1 mark]* — it produces a much smaller file size than the other formats. *[1 mark]*

d) E.g.
• No data is lost when compressed *[1 mark]* so graphics can be reverted back to the original — this is essential to ensure graphics are always high quality. *[1 mark]*
• File sizes are only slightly reduced *[1 mark]* so there would be an impact on storage requirements to the company. *[1 mark]*
• Not all software is compatible with lossless file types *[1 mark]* so clients may not be able to open graphics. *[1 mark]*
• File sizes are large *[1 mark]* so the images will take longer to upload or attach to emails for clients. *[1 mark]*
[6 marks available in total]

Answers